pathways

a guided workbook for youth beginning treatment

Revised Edition

Timothy J. Kahn

SaferSocietyPress

P. O. Box 340
Brandon, VT 05733-0340

Editors: Euan Bear & Fay Honey Knopp

ISBN 1-884444-34-2

$15.00
Bulk discounts available

Order from:

The Safer Society Press
P. O. Box 340
Brandon, VT 05733-0340
(802) 247-3132

Also available:
Pathways Guide for Parents of Youth Beginning Treatment, $8.00 each

ALL ORDERS MUST BE PREPAID, U.S. FUNDS ONLY
Phone orders accepted with VISA or MasterCard
Vermont residents, please add sales tax

ACKNOWLEDGMENTS

Pathways is based on work that has been done in several well known treatment programs for adolescent sexual offenders in Washington State. The many staff members at Echo Glen Children's Center, a state correctional institution operated by Washington's Division of Juvenile Rehabilitation, deserve particular recognition. Echo Glen was one of the first correctional institutions in the United States to offer specialized treatment services to adolescent sexual offenders. Special credit goes to James Giles, Mary Lafond, Greg Merrill, Randy Green, Shelley Ronnfeldt, Joe Loutey, Judy Talton, Nancy German, and Heather Chambers for their encouragement and ongoing dedication to providing quality treatment services to adolescent sexual offenders. I would also like to thank Julie Blackburn and Karen Brunson for their early encouragement and work in this field.

Many professional associates have provided valuable input and feedback about *Pathways* since it was first published. I would like to particularly thank my associate Greg Hunter for his hard work and thoughtful comments. Staff members at the Friends of Youth Griffin Home have also worked hard to incorporate *Pathways* into their program, and have provided excellent ideas about how to improve it. The probation staff at the King County Department of Youth Services have also been very supportive and helpful.

My heartfelt thanks go to my wife, DeeAnn, who helped me find the time necessary to complete this project.

In addition to the friends and colleagues listed above, Robert Freeman-Longo, who pioneered the concept of guided workbooks for adult sexual offenders and assisted greatly in the development of *Pathways*, deserves a great deal of credit and has my deepest appreciation. Thanks also to David Finkelhor of the Family Violence Research Program at the University of New Hampshire for the use of his "Four Preconditions" theory and for his helpful comments; to Jan Hindman for the use of her "Restitution Model" for offender-victim interactions from *Just Before Dawn* (1989, AlexAndria Associates); and to Jonathan Ross, Peter Loss and the offenders in the Forensic Mental Health Services Program for use of their 12 Steps for Sex Offenders. Without the honest and insightful critiques and comments by Connie Isaac (then of Redirecting Sexual Aggression, currently the Executive Director of the Association for the Treatment of Sexual Abusers) and Alison Stickrod Gray of the Vermont Center for Prevention Services, *Pathways* would be a far less universal and helpful workbook.

I also give my thanks and respect to the hundreds of adolescent sex offenders who had the courage and commitment to admit their sexual offenses and participate in stressful and difficult treatment programs such as those described in this workbook. A sexual offender in today's society faces embarrassment, rejection, anger, and hatred, making honest disclosure and treatment a scary experience. Adolescent sexual offenders who can stand up to their mistakes and attempt to make amends to the people they have hurt deserve our support and understanding. With intensive and specialized treatment there is hope that they can change their sexual behavior and stop their developing pattern of abuse.

This workbook is dedicated to all teenage sex offenders who find the strength and motivation to work in treatment on addressing the problem areas that contribute to their offending behavior.

Foreword To Counselors and Group Leaders

Thank you for using *Pathways: A Guided Workbook for Youth Beginning Treatment* in your adolescent sex-offender treatment group. This workbook brings together components from several programs and will help your clients benefit from treatment. The completed *Pathways* workbook gives your clients a resource they can refer to after they make the transition from initial treatment into long-term treatment or aftercare monitoring.

Pathways is *not* a comprehensive program description. The exercises are designed to complement a well-structured counseling/group therapy program. It will be most useful when introduced early in the course of treatment for adolescent sex offenders. Please use the chapters in whatever order suits your program. A packet of tests has been developed by author Tim Kahn to help you assess your clients' grasp of the material presented in each chapter. The test packet is available from the author (515 116th Avenue NE, Suite 145, Bellevue, WA 98004).

Sex offender programs appear to differ in the way they treat issues of confidentiality,[1] one of the thorniest issues facing treatment providers. The problem is how to make a counseling group safe enough for the offenders to disclose the full extent of their aggression while holding them legally accountable and making services available to previously unacknowledged victims.

In general, clinicians should clarify with clients in advance what they are required by law to do regarding disclosure of additional unreported offenses. Disclosure of *all* offenses is always encouraged so that offenders will be held accountable, changes in offenders' risk levels can be assessed, and victims may get help. But misunderstandings between clients and group leaders may destroy trust and set treatment back. *Pathways* allows young offenders to complete the homework assignments using only the first names of unreported victims, giving clinicians a window into the offender's previously undisclosed behavior and a way of supporting eventual full disclosure and accountability. The *Pathways* approach should be modified in accordance with your program's guidelines.

In the growing field of adolescent sex-offender treatment, divergent theoretical models and treatment rationales continue to emerge. Clinicians may disagree on the proper sequence and timing of different treatment components, especially when dealing with the offender's possible past experience as a victim of physical or sexual abuse. Some clinicians address the offender's victimization early in treatment as a tool to build empathy skills for the later clarification process. They reason that the offender's feelings may remain blocked or frozen until the early abuse is recognized, acknowledged, and worked on. Other treatment providers deal with their clients' past victimization experiences much later because they feel it distracts sex offenders from their primary work of accepting responsibility for their aggressive behaviors and learning to control them. In their experience, sex offenders often see early victimization as the "cause" of their abusive behavior.

---

[1] *The Revised Report from the National Task Force on Juvenile Sex Offending (1993) of the National Adolescent Perpetrator Network*, with a few dissenting opinions, advises against extending absolute therapeutic confidentiality to sex offenders, "because it promotes the secrecy which supports sexual abuse and may endanger the community." The majority of juvenile sex offender treatment programs require clients to sign a waiver of client-therapist confidentiality regarding previously undisclosed sex offenses (see p. 22, Assumptions 54-56, and p. 37, Assumption 121).

The recommendations of *dissenting* National Task Force members range from honoring full confidentiality to using sign releases for specific information to be given to *named* cooperating agenciesrather than a blanket waiver. Without some measure of confidentiality, the dissenters reason, offenders have little incentive to disclose their complete sexual histories, and their true risk levels may not be clearly discerned by clinicians (see p. 97, Assumptions 121& 220 for dissents).

Pathways takes the middle course on this issue by introducing victim empathy (Chapter Four, Learning About Victims) early — immediately after the sexual offense disclosure chapter. Some clients may disclose histories of abuse at this point. The young offender's work on identifying the abusive thoughts, feelings, and behaviors leading to sexual aggression (Chapters Five – Seven) and descriptions of intervention techniques and relapse prevention (Chapters Eight and Nine) come before the offender's potential history as a victim of abuse (Chapter Ten) — building victim empathy for the clarification process that follows in Chapter Eleven. Clinicians have reported receiving disclosures of past abuse at each of these points.

Because the assault cycle is so widely used in sex-offender treatment programs, and to supplement your program's intensive group work on the elements of the cycle itself, *Pathways* concentrates on the "thinking errors"[2] that offenders use to move from one part of their cycle to the next (Chapter Seven).

Since *Pathways* is designed to be used early in the treatment process, Chapter Eight *describes* but *does not teach* selected impulse- and arousal-control intervention techniques. The text further cautions young offenders that they must be supervised and monitored by an experienced sex-offender treatment provider in order to use them. Controversy surrounds the use of some arousal-control techniques with juveniles, especially Masturbation Satiation. Many clinicians are understandably reluctant to use this technique because little is known about the consequences of attempts to change adolescent arousal patterns.

Because program models differ, Relapse Prevention is taught as a series of techniques rather than as an overall integrated theoretical model. Clients are instructed to identify their "warning signs" and high risk situations and develop multiple appropriate coping strategies. They contract with significant others (family, teachers, probation officials) to support their efforts at preventing reoffense.

The chapter adapted from 12-Step self-help models (Chapter Twelve) is intended to be used much later in treatment. It can provide a good structure for clients' transition into the aftercare component of a treatment program and introduces the idea of continuing post-transition self-monitoring. Many programs using addiction or medical models to address sexual offending behavior adopt AA-type language regarding the "recovery" process. Because "recovery" seems to conflict with the message that sexual offending has no "cure" — only *control* — in *Pathways,* young offenders are encouraged to adopt a "sexual abuse prevention and safety lifestyle," and become a member of the "prevention and safety team."

Treatment of juvenile sex offenders is a rapidly evolving field, and we welcome your comments on the content and format of *Pathways*. Thanks for your work with this difficult and potentially rewarding population. Each adolescent sex offender responding to your treatment may save hundreds of potential victims from a lifetime of trauma. We salute your efforts and again thank you for using *Pathways.*

Two Pathways Exercises

Two exercises have scorable answers: Chapter 1, Legal/Illegal Behaviors, and Chapter 13, Adolescent Sexual Information Scale (ASIS). Suggested answers and scoring key are included below.

LEGAL/ILLEGAL BEHAVIOR

These answers are based on sexual assault laws common in the U.S. and Canada in 1996. Sexual assault laws in individual states and provinces may vary widely. Consult an attorney, juvenile court worker, or counselor for information about specific laws in your area. *Due to the variation in the*

---

[2] Yochelson, S. & Samenow, S. (1976-77). *The Criminal Personality,* Vol. I & II. Dunmore, PA: Jason Aronson.

laws of differing jurisdictions, some answers provided below may be inaccurate in some locations. Since it was intended to promote discussion, answers are not provided for the *coercion* vs. *consent* question.

1. Jack's behavior is illegal. The behavior described is clearly rape. Since Jack removed Linda's clothes against her will while she tried to get him to stop, an argument may be made that some force was used. Except in states where there is no law against rape between married partners, Jack's behavior is legally considered rape because Linda clearly expressed her lack of consent.

2. Tony's behavior is probably legal, assuming that his girlfriend consented and was a willing partner in the sexual encounter. Since there appears to be only a two-year age difference, this would most likely not be considered Statutory Rape. It could, of course, be considered indecent exposure if someone saw them undressed or having sex in the park.

3. Jeannie's behavior is illegal. Her behavior could be charged as several crimes, including Child Molestation, Communicating with a Minor for Immoral Purposes, or Indecent Exposure. Since there is more than a four-year age difference and the boy is only ten years old, it doesn't matter that he appeared to go along with it — he is well under the statutory age of consent.

4. Maria's behavior is illegal. Her behavior could be charged as Statutory Rape or Communicating with a Minor for Immoral Purposes. Since Booker is younger than the statutory age of consent, it doesn't matter that he appeared to go along with the sexual behavior.

5. Bill's behavior is illegal. He could be charged with Rape, Child Molestation or Communicating with a Minor for Immoral Purposes. Since Bill tried to put his penis in Cindy's vagina, he could be charged with Rape. Because Rape includes any penetration, no matter how slight, it doesn't matter that his penis wouldn't go all the way in.

6. Scott's behavior is illegal. Because of the age difference, he could be charged with Child Molestation.

7. Hank's behavior is probably legal, assuming of course, that both boys gave their consent.

8. Dan's behavior is illegal. He could be charged with Rape. It doesn't matter that Barbara, his victim, didn't tell for two weeks. Victims often postpone reporting because of embarrassment, shame, and fear of being revictimized by the court process.

9. Sam's behavior is illegal. He could be charged with Rape, Incest, or perhaps even Assault.

10. Charles's behavior is illegal, even though Susan appeared to give her consent and was a willing participant in the sexual encounter. Since Susan was under the age of consent (16), and Charles was more than two years older, he could be charged with Statutory Rape, Child Molestation, or Communicating with a Minor for Immoral Purposes.

11. Jamie's and Marcus's behavior is most likely illegal because they disseminated pornography involving sexual images of children to younger children without their knowledge. They could be charged with Communicating with a Minor for Immoral Purposes.

CHAPTER 13: ADOLESCENT SEXUAL INFORMATION SURVEY

This test isn't scored by comparing a total score to ranges. Each question may indicate a thinking error contributing to the adolescent offender's aggressive sexual behavior. **Score each question individually.**

To score the test, use the following key: Questions 1, 4, 6, 9, 12, 17, 18, and 23 are scored in reverse (1 = 5, 2 = 4, 3 = 3, 4 = 2, 5 = 1). All other questions are scored normally (1 = 1, 5 = 5). After converting the scores, **look for low numbers (1, 2, 3), indicating potential thinking errors or lack of knowledge about sexual victimization or offending behavior.**

TABLE OF CONTENTS

CHAPTER	TITLE	PAGE

INTRODUCTION TO THE REVISED EDITION

Welcome to *Pathways*, your guided treatment workbook for helping you change your problem sexual behaviors. *Pathways* provides you with a step-by-step manual for understanding and changing sexual behavior that hurts other people and gets you in trouble. This workbook is a starting point and helpful addition to treatment. You must remember, however, that change is hard work, and your counselor and treatment group will be your guides, along with *Pathways*. This workbook cannot replace specialized sexual deviancy counseling by trained professionals, but it may help you better understand how to make the changes in your life that will keep your problem sexual behaviors under control. In *Pathways*, you will learn new and non-hurtful ways of dealing with your feelings, thoughts, and behavior patterns. By working through *Pathways* you will become a lifetime member of the sexual abuse prevention team.

Sexual abuse is a huge problem in our society. Thousands of people just like you have committed sexual offenses, or have been in trouble for their problem sexual behavior. More than half the child molestation cases reported to the police are committed by teenagers. Some teenagers even kill innocent victims, or cause serious physical harm that requires that the victim go to a hospital. Even simple touching of a child's private parts can be very frightening and upsetting for the child and the child's family. So, no matter what *your* sexual behavior problem might be, it is important to remember that most people consider it to be a very serious matter. Sometimes you might feel alone, or like you are the only person who has done these things. Certainly, it is very frightening, embarrassing, and confusing to be confronted about sexual behavior. Remember though, *you are not alone,* even though you might sometimes feel alone. By completing *Pathways* you will become a member of the sexual abuse prevention team, and will learn a new way of life. This workbook will help you develop "hip-pocket" tools that you can use everyday to develop a healthy and sex-offense free lifestyle. By making these changes and doing this work, you will earn the respect of your family and everybody else involved in your life.

Pathways is written for both boys and girls. While there are more boys than girls in treatment for committing sex offenses, the process is very similar for both. This latest revision of *Pathways* tries to balance the exercises and examples so that both boys and girls in treatment are described.

This revised edition of *Pathways* contains new information and exercises about victims, as well as a new long-range prevention plan assignment to help you learn how to stay *sex offense free* long after you finish therapy. There is also some new information about arousal control, to help you learn to control your sexual feelings in a positive way. Also, since some of you are dating now or are planning to start dating, there is a new section on handling social relationships to help you decide when and if you should tell a girlfriend or boyfriend about your problem sexual behavior.

Consider these remarks by Rachel, a 17-year-old girl on probation for a sex offense:

> *Pathways* is a book for sex offenders who are stuck into denial, or want help in their treatment. This book includes the steps to safety and prevention: sex offense cycles, prevention plans, warning signals, and many other helpful steps. If you want what is offered in this book then you will work through it and deal with the frustration, the emotions, and the work that is required.

Or these comments from Steven, a 15-year-old sex offender:

> Why should sex offenders need or get involved in treatment? The reason is because sex offenders need to take care of their feelings in a positive way. An offender needs to attend a group to deal with his/her past, present, and future life. It will help, because he/she is getting feelings out on the table. Treatment will only work if the offender is willing to learn.

Pathways is most useful when you combine your work on its assignments with your work in therapy and/or in an adolescent sex offenders' treatment group. It is designed to help you talk about your problems with aggressive sexuality and to give you information that will help you control your problem behaviors. To help you get the most benefit from reading this book, your counselor may give you tests on each chapter. You will do well on the tests if you read each chapter carefully and ask questions about anything you don't understand. Completing *Pathways* will not "cure" you of your problem sexual behaviors—there is no cure—but it will teach you how to recognize and control them.

Since all teenage sex offenders are different and have varying levels of education and ability, some parts of the workbook may seem too hard or too easy for you. This is to be expected—it is up to you to do your best by asking for help from others or doing extra work as necessary. Since many of the assignments involve rewriting, it may be easier to do them on a computer, if there's one you can use.

Good luck in traveling your path to safety and in joining the sexual abuse prevention team!

Timothy J. Kahn
Bellevue, Washington

THE PREVENTION & SAFETY PATH

As you progress along your path of prevention and safety, fill in the footprint after each chapter or step assignment you have completed and had approved by your counselor or treatment group. While completing *Pathways* indicates you have made treatment progress, it does not guarantee that your problem areas are completely resolved. Prevention is an ongoing way of life.

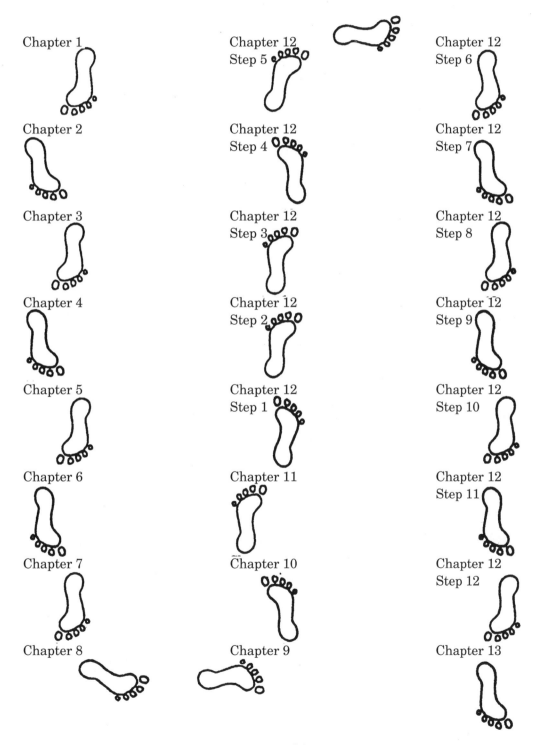

Chapter 1

Chapter 2

Chapter 3

Chapter 4

Chapter 5

Chapter 6

Chapter 7

Chapter 8

Chapter 12
Step 5

Chapter 12
Step 4

Chapter 12
Step 3

Chapter 12
Step 2

Chapter 12
Step 1

Chapter 11

Chapter 10

Chapter 9

Chapter 12
Step 6

Chapter 12
Step 7

Chapter 12
Step 8

Chapter 12
Step 9

Chapter 12
Step 10

Chapter 12
Step 11

Chapter 12
Step 12

Chapter 13

CHAPTER ONE

COURT, EVALUATION, AND INITIAL REACTIONS

If you have gone to juvenile court for any type of offense, you know how scary and upsetting it can be. Laws and court rules can be very complex and confusing. In most states and provinces, a teenager charged with a sexual offense must go through several court appearances, called "hearings." Sometimes, though, a teenager may only talk with an attorney and not go into a courtroom at all.

Listen for a moment to Kim, a 13-year-old girl who has recently finished *Pathways:*

> For me, my sexual problems started when I was molested and raped by my biological father. I was about 5 years old at the time. At that time I went to counseling to help me understand that what happened to me wasn't my fault and that I couldn't have really prevented it. After about two years of counseling, my counselor thought I had learned how to deal with the abuse. I realize now that I really didn't know everything I needed to know. Silly me, I still thought to myself that I could have prevented my dad from sexually abusing me. Even after counseling I had dreams and flashbacks about the abuse, and I tried to push them away.

> After I hit puberty when I was about 12, my dreams and flashbacks came back, and were even more confusing. I also had new sexual feelings that I didn't really understand. I kept those feelings a secret, and tried to forget them. That's when all the trouble hit, because the feelings got too strong for me to handle and I sexually offended my younger brother who was eight years old. Actually, I know now that I *can* handle my feelings. I noticed that my brother was curious about things, and I thought that would make it easy for me to do sexual things to him. I tried to stop offending, but I really didn't know how. I ended up offending him many times. I stopped eating, and I started feeling very sick and guilty. The best thing I did was to finally tell my mother what I did. After that I started counseling again, and I was taken out of my home for several days. Then my family and I went through months of court meetings, appointments with counselors and lawyers, questions, and tests. In *Pathways* you will be asked to uncover your feelings, and tell some of them to others. If you are at all like me, this is hard. In the end it is for the best. During that time I often doubted that it would ever end, and I sometimes thought that maybe I shouldn't have told what I did.

> Since that time I have finished *Pathways* and I am practicing what I have learned in order to live a healthier life. My brother has been to counseling, and we have talked about what I did to him. I made it through the court process, and I feel much, much better about myself now. I truly had no idea a year ago how my behavior could affect so many other people. No matter what you have done in the past, I hope that you are brave and strong enough to hold your head up and tell the complete truth about everything you have done, and everything you feel. This is important, no matter how hard it might be for you. For me, keeping secrets was my greatest mistake, other than sexually abusing my brother. For me my greatest success was admitting my mistakes and earning the respect and forgiveness of others. If I can make it through this, you can too. Everybody's story is different, and I have met teenagers with sexual problems who have *not* been abused like I was. So take charge and control of your life, and remember that it is up to you to make your story have a happy ending.

An early step in taking charge of your behavior change is learning what behaviors are illegal and wrong. Different states and provinces have different laws and categories of sexual offenses. Talk with your counselor to help you understand the laws where you live. *Remember, the laws in your state or province may be different from those listed below. Ask your counselor or probation/parole officer for a copy of the laws that apply to you. When you complete the assignment in this chapter, you should use the laws that apply in your state or province.* Below is a general list of several different types of sexual offense laws that may apply to you.

Indecent Exposure: When a person makes an obscene exposure in public of any private parts such as a penis, vagina, breasts, or anus (bottom), it is a crime. Usually, it is treated as a more serious crime when the victim is under age 14. For example, a teenager who shows his penis to a child would be charged with Indecent Exposure.

Obscene Phone Calls/Peeping: In most places it is against the law to call someone on the telephone to say sexual things to them without their consent. It is also against the law to peek into people's windows or otherwise violate their private living space.

Child Molestation: Child molestation refers to any sexual contact with a child. In most areas, if you are a teenager, it is illegal to have sex with a person if he/she is three or more years younger than you. "Sexual contact" includes sexual intercourse, touching a child's breasts, kissing "private parts" (penis, vagina, anus, etc.), or masturbating onto them. Children may *say* it is okay to do sexual things with them, but legally and morally it is the older person's responsibility to know what is right (safe and protective) and wrong (hurtful). It is illegal and wrong to have sexual contact with any child three or more years younger, even if they appear to go along with it.

Communicating with a Minor for Immoral Purposes: This crime may be called by other names in different parts of the U.S. and Canada. You can be charged with this type of crime any time you talk with or show pictures to anyone under age 18 if the communication is sexual in nature. For example, if you show a pornographic magazine to a child you could be charged with this crime. If you download pornographic images from the Internet to your computer and then send them or print them out and show them to younger children, you could be charged. Laws restricting pornography on the Internet are still being made but some people have already been arrested under existing laws by being tracked through their online services. It is "immoral communicating" when an older person *asks* a child to have sex with him/her, whether or not the sex act is attempted or completed. Sometimes, a sex offender is charged with this type of crime when the more serious crime of child molestation cannot be proven.

Incest: Most states and provinces consider it a serious crime to have sexual contact with someone who is closely related to you. This includes brothers, sisters, children, and stepchildren.

Rape: A sexual act is rape whenever a person has sexual intercourse with someone against that person's will. It is rape any time force or weapons are used or threatened, or the victim is injured. The victim doesn't have to fight back for it to be rape—all a person has to do is say, "no." Rape can include *any penetration of any body part* (mouth, anus, vagina) by any of the offender's body parts or by an object, not just putting a penis in a vagina. For example, if you put your finger even part way in a girl's vagina or a boy's anus you can be charged with rape. Any penetration is considered rape. ***Sodomy*** (pronounced sod-o-me) is anal rape (putting a penis, other body part, or object in another person's anus or bottom).

Statutory Rape: Statutory rape laws define how old a person has to be before he or she can be considered able to legally consent to participate in a sexual act. Sexual contact with anyone under this age, regardless of whether they said it was okay, is automatically considered rape. In most places, it is against the law to have sex with anyone under the age of 16. Normally, the law allows sexual contact between two teenagers who are about the same age (within two years), as long as both persons want to have the sexual contact and no force, tricks, bribes, or intimidation are used. If one of the teenagers is more than two years older than the other, and the other teenager is under 16 years old, the older person could be charged with statutory rape.

While the law defines a particular "age of consent," *age* is not the only thing to consider in looking at whether a person has consented to participate in any sexual act. The difference between *coercion, compliance,* or *cooperation*, and *consent* is important, too.

Coercion: Using tricks, bribes, force, threats, or intimidation to get someone to go along with what you want to do. Coercion is the tool you use to get victims to comply or cooperate.

Compliance: When victims simply go along without actively resisting even though they may think it is wrong and don't want to participate.

Cooperation: When a victim participates regardless of whether he/she wants to or thinks it is right.

Victims may comply or cooperate without having given *consent*.

Consent: When a partner agrees with an action. The partner must *understand* the proposed action, *know* what society's standards are for this action, *be aware* of the consequences and alternatives, *be assured* that a decision to disagree will be respected as much as a decision to agree, *voluntarily agree*, and be *mentally competent*.

The name or title of the law you are charged with breaking may not have anything to do with what you actually did. Prosecutors usually file the most serious charge they feel they can prove, but they will sometimes accept a guilty plea to a reduced charge in order to avoid putting a victim through a painful, costly, and time-consuming trial. If your case is "plea-bargained," the name of the charge you eventually plead guilty to or are convicted of will influence the type of sentence you receive. In treatment, however, you should **describe your actual sexual behavior** rather than giving the legal name of your crime.

While you are going through the court process, the advice of your attorney is intended to protect your rights and help you receive the best possible sentence. Your attorney is not a counselor, however, and may not know much about the treatment you need as a sex offender. Sometimes you may be faced with a difficult decision: "Do I tell the truth about what I did or do I keep my mouth shut to try to get a lighter sentence?" You are the only one who can make that decision. You have to live with yourself. In treatment, **honesty counts**—it is the only way to get help for you and for your victims.

As you prepare for an evaluation by a psychologist or social worker, remember **you are not alone!** Thousands of other teenagers have been through exactly what you are going through. They've made it, and many of them got enough help and worked hard to keep from ever offending again. It is normal to be scared and upset during this time. Some people you meet will act unfriendly and rejecting. You will also meet people who truly want to help you and will not reject you. The nature of the court process is that people tend to take different sides, and the judge has to decide what is best for you, best for your victims, and best for the community.

Listen to Jeff, a 16-year-old sex offender, talk about his experiences during the evaluation and court process:

> It was about eight times scarier than anything I ever did before. It was the first time anybody had ever heard what I did. I had to tell the truth because they'd know if I was lying. When you go through evaluation they are getting into private stuff that you don't want to tell them. My first response to their questions was, "I don't know." They'd always catch it and I would eventually end up telling the truth.

After I told the truth it wasn't nearly as hard as I thought it would be. Actually it turned out to be a lot easier to tell the evaluators what I did than it was to tell my family. My counselors helped me talk to my parents after the evaluation was completed. My advice to other teenage sex offenders is to relax, as tough as that will be. It will make it easier if you tell the truth. In the end you'll get caught up in your lies anyway.

During the evaluation process the counselor or psychologist doing the interviewing and testing will ask you lots of hard questions that you may never have been asked before. You will be asked personal questions about your family, school, work, friends, and your sexual history. You will be asked questions that you don't think are important or even related to what you did. During this process it is important to *listen carefully to each question*, and *answer as honestly as possible*. Lying only makes things worse. In most cases it is best to get everything out during the evaluation. If you have more victims or have committed more incidents of abuse than people know about, admit it now and get it behind you so treatment can begin. If you admit to your mistakes now, the judge may be easier on you. If your behavior is discovered by someone else telling about it, the judge may not be so understanding.

You will also be asked to complete lots of different paper-and-pencil tests. Sometimes you will get to take them home to work on. One of the easiest things you can do to help yourself at this stage is to finish the tasks and get them back to the evaluator on time. By doing that, you send a clear message that you are serious about evaluation and treatment, making it more likely that your sentence will be more about treatment and less about punishment. Juvenile courts want to make sure that you get help for your problems, and that nobody else will be hurt by you. If you are sincere about getting help, the court may decide it does not need to lock you up to protect the community.

Assignment #1-A: Legal/Illegal Behavior. Read each of the scenes below carefully, then decide if the behavior described is legal or illegal, according to the definitions in this chapter. If you know what the specific laws are in your state or province, answer the questions with them in mind.

1. Jack, a 20-year-old, has been living with Linda, who is 19, for two years. One evening Linda fixes Jack a romantic dinner with candlelight and soft music. After dinner Jack and Linda put their infant son to bed. Soon afterward Jack starts caressing and kissing Linda. As Jack's kissing becomes more intense, Linda asks him to stop—the baby might wake up. Jack continues despite her objections and begins removing her clothes. Linda again asks Jack to stop, but he doesn't.

   _____Jack's behavior is legal

   _____Jack's behavior is illegal

   Name the illegal behavior:_____

   Was there [circle one] **coercion** or **consent**? (Remember, *consent* involves more than just saying "yes." See page 14 for definitions of *coercion* and *consent*.)

2. Tony, age 15, is in the ninth grade. One warm night after taking Margreta, his 13-year-old girlfriend, to a school dance, he walks her home through the neighborhood park where they playfully wrestle on the grass. They end up making love in the park, then Tony walks Margreta home.

   _____Tony's behavior is legal

   _____Tony's behavior is illegal

   Name the illegal behavior:_____

   Was there [circle one] **coercion** or **consent** ?

3. Jeannie, who is 14, has been babysitting for the Ramirez family for two years. While Jeannie is babysitting 10-year-old Victor, she notices his erection and asks him to show it to her. He happily agrees. Jeannie then takes down her pants and asks Victor to touch her private parts. He agrees.

_____Jeannie's behavior is legal

_____Jeannie's behavior is illegal

Name the illegal behavior: _____

Was there [circle one] **coercion** or **consent** ?

4. Maria, who is 20, lives alone in an apartment downstairs from Booker, a 15-year-old freshman in high school. One evening when Booker comes by to collect for his paper route, Maria invites him in while she looks for her purse. When she comes back her blouse is unbuttoned and she starts acting seductive towards Booker. Maria starts fondling Booker and they end up having intercourse.

_____Maria's behavior is legal

_____Maria's behavior is illegal

Name the illegal behavior:_____

Was there [circle one] **coercion** or **consent** ?

5. Bill, age 14, is pretty popular with the kids in his neighborhood. He often babysits to earn extra money. One night he feels turned on by Cindy, the 7-year-old he is babysitting. He talks her into having sex with him, but his penis won't fit all the way into her vagina.

_____Bill's behavior is legal

_____Bill's behavior is illegal

Name the illegal behavior:_____

Was there [circle one] **coercion** or **consent** ?

6. Scott, age 12, likes to play with younger children in the neighborhood. One day he goes out to his treehouse with his friend Jason, age 8. After looking at pictures and cartoons in some Playboy magazines together they masturbate each other.

_____Scott's behavior is legal

_____Scott's behavior is illegal

Name the illegal behavior:_____

Was there [circle one] **coercion** or **consent** ?

7. Hank and Jeremy, both 15 and members of the sophomore class, are good friends who like to spend time together. One evening at Hank's home they end up masturbating each other and having anal intercourse using condoms.

_____Hank's behavior is legal

_____Hank's behavior is illegal

Name the illegal behavior:_____

Was there [circle one] **coercion** or **consent** ?

8. Dan is 14, very popular, and has lots of girlfriends. One day he and two of his 16-year-old friends pick up Barbara, a girl he knows a little from his homeroom in school. They drive to a park, where Dan threatens Barbara with his knife so she'll have sex with him. She doesn't say anything about it to anybody for nearly two weeks.

    _____Dan's behavior is legal

    _____Dan's behavior is illegal

    Name the illegal behavior:_____

    Was there [circle one] **coercion** or **consent** ?

9. Sam, age 13, lives with his mother and Alice, his retarded 25-year-old stepsister. One evening while alone with Alice, he forces her to rub his penis. She tries to get away but he holds her down.

    _____Sam's behavior is legal

    _____Sam's behavior is illegal

    Name the illegal behavior:_____

    Was there [circle one] **coercion** or **consent** ?

10. Charles is 17 and has been going out for two months with Susan, age 13. Coming home one evening after a movie, they find nobody home at Susan's. They watch TV for a while and start to kiss and fondle each other. They end up having intercourse on the living room floor.

    _____Charles' behavior is legal

    _____Charles' behavior is illegal

    Name the illegal behavior:_____

    Was there [circle one] **coercion** or **consent** ?

11. 12-year-old Jamie and 13-year-old Marcus figured out how to get pornography off the Internet and to send it via E-mail to their friends 9-year-old Roderick and 10-year-old Jose. Roderick and Jose did not know anything about the pictures being sent to them. Some of the pictures involved little kids in sexual situations.

    _____Jamie's and Marcus's behavior is legal

    _____Jamie's and Marcus's behavior is illegal

    Name the illegal behavior:_____

    Was there [circle one] **coercion** or **consent**?

Your counselor can check your answers and help clear up any confusion you have over issues of coercion and consent.

POWER AND CONTROL

So far, this chapter has been about looking at legal and illegal behavior. You have acted out illegal sexual behavior. But committing a crime and being caught are only the last steps in your offense. Your illegal sexual behavior starts with feelings, thoughts, and actions that aren't illegal, though they're harmful to you and others around you.

Your treatment is aimed at helping you control your illegal behavior by changing your behavior, thoughts, and feelings that are harmful. The first step in changing is identifying your harmful behaviors. *Harmful behavior* is any behavior that treats another person like a *thing* instead of a real human being. *Harmful behavior* is also self-centered behavior. When you were having problems with your sexual behavior, you were only thinking about *yourself*, and what felt good for you. If you were truly thinking about what was best for the person you abused, you would not have acted out sexually. So, sex offending is all about being self-centered, and a big part of treatment involves learning how to respect the feelings, bodies, and belongings of other people. In Chapter Four you will learn about how to do this by learning to understand *boundaries*, or imaginary walls that keep us safe and protected.

Your offending behavior may be a way for you to meet personal needs that haven't been met any other way. It is *not* wrong for you to have unmet needs. What's wrong is choosing a method for meeting those needs that is harmful to you and to others. Everybody has unmet needs, but most people do not commit sex offenses.

Sometimes you may be feeling helpless or really bad about yourself. You have a need to feel better. The method you choose is making someone else do sexual things with you. You may try to "get even" or feel powerful by being in control of someone else and having a secret about your illegal sexual behavior. When you do that, you are treating the other person like a thing instead of a person.

There are healthy ways to have power. Healthy uses of power always respect the personal rights of other people. *Assertive* people use healthy power. *Assertiveness* is being able to say, "What I feel is is_____. What I want is_____. What I'm willing to do is_____."[1] Assertive people using healthy power accept and respect the other person's answers to those questions.

Assignment #1-B. What is healthy power? Who are your heroes (real people or characters in books or on TV) who use healthy power?

_____

_____

_____

_____

_____

_____

_____

_____

_____

_____

If you need more space, use a separate piece of paper.

---

[1]Thanks to Alison Stickrod Gray for this discussion of assertiveness.

Assignment #1-C. What are some examples of unhealthy power? Who can you think of (real people or TV characters) who uses power in unhealthy ways?

_____

_____

_____

_____

_____

_____

_____

_____

_____

_____

_____

_____

_____

_____

If you need more space, use a separate piece of paper.

Assignment #1-D. What behaviors do you use to get power? Are they healthy or unhealthy? To decide whether they are healthy or unhealthy, ask yourself, "Whose needs was I meeting? Were my actions respectful of the other person's personal rights?"

_____

_____

_____

_____

_____

_____

_____

_____

_____

If you need more space, use a separate piece of paper.

CHAPTER TWO

YOUR TREATMENT GOALS AND BECOMING A GROUP MEMBER

Treatment is something that sounds good but is sometimes hard to explain. While there are lots of experts around and nobody has yet developed a "cure," treatment can teach you how to *control* your sexually harmful behaviors. There is no research proving that one particular method works better than others, but experienced counselors rely on certain methods and goals that seem to be successful with teenage sex offenders. Read and think about each of the treatment goals listed below:

TREATMENT GOALS

1. I will accept full responsibility for my sexually abusive and criminal behavior.

2. I will develop a clear understanding and sensitivity to the effects of sexual abuse on the people I abused.

3. I will develop an understanding of the thoughts and feelings that led to my offenses and identify my pre-offense pattern and offense cycle.

4. I will learn to meet my sexual and social needs without hurting others.

5. I will increase my appropriate sexual arousal and decrease my deviant sexual arousal.

6. I will identify high-risk situations that could lead me to further sexual offending.

7. I will develop an offense prevention plan which other people in my support system will read and sign.

8. I will learn and demonstrate responsible day-to-day behavior which includes avoiding high-risk situations.

Pathways defines treatment as "any activity that brings you closer to meeting these goals." Most treatment programs for teenage sex offenders use peer treatment groups. Groups help sex offenders feel more accepted and less like they are the only ones with this type of problem. Since groups are used so often in treatment, this chapter will teach you some skills for being an involved, active group participant. Following the guidelines below will help your treatment group work effectively.

BECOMING A GOOD GROUP MEMBER

Group therapy can be kind of scary at first, but most teenage sex offenders quickly find that it helps to be able to talk with other teenagers with similar problems. Listen to what it was like for Andrew, who had never been in a therapy group before:

> Group was embarrassing at first. I was scared of telling people about what I had done. Group was scary because I didn't know the people in the group. It was also weird. I wasn't used to talking about my offenses because I didn't want to talk about them. So, when I went into the room with the other members, I lied about masturbation, offending against certain people, and about how many victims I had. But after I got used to people in the group, I started to tell the truth. Now

the group is a place where I can really share my feelings with others, and I get a lot of support and good feelings. My treatment would not have been nearly as effective without the group's help.

The guidelines below will help you be a positive and supportive group therapy participant.

Group Guidelines

1. *Never ask a yes/no question (it makes it too easy for the person to deny or cop-out by saying no).* Denial is a powerful force with sex offenders, so the therapy group should try to make it as easy as possible for each offender to talk about what he/she has done. Suppose a person had five victims, but only got caught for one. If a group member asks, "Do you have any more victims?" it may be hard to answer honestly. On the other hand, if the person is asked, "How many other victims do you have?" the offender has permission and support for telling the truth.

2. *Don't rescue by answering for another member.* Always let people answer for and defend themselves. If someone always answers for you, it is easy to avoid difficult questions. In a therapy group, each person has to do his/her own work.

3. *Always look at the person you are talking to.* Speak up so everyone can hear you clearly. An important part of group therapy is learning to communicate directly with other people. Every time you are talking about someone, you should be looking at them and speaking directly to them. For example, instead of saying, "I think Jon is doing a nice job," look at him and say, "Jon, I think you are doing a nice job."

4. *Always confront thinking errors.* As you will learn in *Pathways,* thinking errors help you commit sex offenses. If you let a group member use a thinking error, you are letting him/her continue to act in a way that could lead to further offenses. This type of behavior is called *enabling. Enabling* is when you help another person avoid the consequences of his/her behavior.

5. *Support other people when they need encouragement.* Support is one of the most important things in a therapy group. Talking in a group, especially about sexual matters, is very hard. Every group member needs to work hard to develop trust and a supportive feeling in the group. A simple way to be supportive is to always greet each group member by name, and say positive things to others.

6. *Pay attention, don't start side conversations.* A therapy group is defined as two or more persons who are working together to resolve problems they have in common. In group therapy everyone concentrates on the one person who is talking. When you start side conversations, the group is no longer working together.

7. *Everybody gets equal time—don't try to dominate the group.* In every therapy group there are active members and passive members. If only the outgoing members were allowed to talk, nobody would get to know the quiet, less active members. In a group, everybody is equal, and even the quietest people should get equal time. Outgoing, talkative members can help support the quieter members in talking.

8. *Get involved, don't expect the group leaders to ask all the questions or do all the work.* The group leader's job is to get all group members participating and helping one another. At first the group leaders will take the lead and teach the group how to help each other. After a few meetings, however, each group member gets involved as much as possible. You have experiences and feelings to share and questions to ask that might help someone else, too.

9. *Sit in an equal circle. Sit straight in your seat; look interested and involved.* These basic rules help each member stay involved in the group. In an equal circle, each group member can see every other group member.

10. *Give honest feedback.* In a therapy group it doesn't help anybody to avoid the truth. Tell it like it is, even if someone may get mad at you or have hurt feelings. In a group, honesty is essential.

11. *Keep it simple, make sure others understand you.* Since there are usually six to twelve other teenagers in a group, it is important that members keep their comments brief and clear. Group members have different abilities, so try to address your comments to the youngest or least able member.

12. *Don't take offense at what people say, keep an open mind.* You will likely get mad at what someone says to you in group. At those times, remind yourself that the group is trying to help you, not hurt you.

13. *Keep what you say and hear in the group confidential!* Nobody likes being known as a sex offender, and what happens in the group should stay in the group. This way the group will be a safe place where people can share their real feelings and thoughts. If you share information with people outside the group, trust will be lost and group therapy will not work.

14. *Let one person talk at a time, don't interrupt.* Maintain respect for all group members. Everybody has something important to say, even if you don't like or agree with it. Wait for a person to finish before jumping in with comments or questions. When in doubt, excuse yourself and ask if the person is finished.

15. *Arrive on time and leave on time.* By arriving on time, you show everybody that you are serious about treatment and that you care about the group. By leaving on time, you give the group leader(s) a chance to plan the next group and talk about what happened in the most recent meeting.

If you keep these guidelines in mind you will contribute to the group's ability to help each member through the difficult treatment process. Each therapy group discusses guidelines such as these and other ways to help the group run well.

You have something else to offer your treatment group: your sharp observations. Your experience can help other members understand how and why they committed their sexual offenses. Because you know what it's like from the inside, you can probably tell when another group member is not telling the whole story, trying to cover something up, or is just too scared to talk straight. You can help by paying close attention to what other group members say and asking them questions about their thoughts and feelings. Below are some examples of good questions to ask in group. You'll probably come up with even better ones on your own.

1. How did you get the people you abused to do what you wanted, how did you "groom" them?

2. What kind of force or threats did you use?

3. How do you think the people you abused were feeling before, during, and after your offenses?

4. How do you feel about your offenses now? Why?

5. Why are you here in this treatment group? What do you want to do?

Avoid asking yes or no questions—they make it too easy for someone to take the easy way out and simply say "no."

MAKING A LIST OF YOUR PROBLEMS AND GOALS

Pathways is written for you as a teenage sex offender, whether your offense involved molesting children, raping peers or adults, obscene phone calls, peeping, or exhibitionism (flashing). Because all sex offenders are different, you must develop a list of problems and goals which apply *only to you*. In order to complete this assignment you have to understand that your sexual problems are connected to other problems in your life—they're not separate. If you are male, your offenses were not caused by an "out of control" penis. If you are female, your sexually aggressive behaviors were not caused by curiosity or "wondering how it would feel." *They were caused by your brain sending messages to other parts of your body to act in certain ways.*

Below is a list of problems and goals that other teenage sex offenders developed during their treatment. Review them to see which ones apply to you. See if you can think of other problems and goals which are not listed that apply to you.

Problems

I feel turned on by young kids.

I don't have any friends my own age.

I don't like asking girls out.

I'm afraid I might be gay/lesbian.

I always get into trouble at school.

I use drugs/alcohol a lot.

I have a mean temper that I can't control.

I am always fighting with my family.

I am depressed and I don't care about anything.

I never get asked out.

I feel like I'm worthless.

I like hurting other people.

I am always bored.

Nobody loves me.

Goals

I want to express my feelings without hurting others.

I want to have a girlfriend/boyfriend my own age.

I want to feel okay about my gay/lesbian feelings.

I want to stop hurting other people.

I want to keep my anger under control.

I want to feel good about who I am.

I want to have good friends who really care.

I want to stop drinking and using drugs.

I want to do better at school.

I want other people to trust and respect me.

Assignment #2: Problems and Goals. Make your own list of problems and goals using the examples as a starting point. Talk with your counselor and parents to get their input. After you develop your list you may be asked to share it with your treatment group. *Save this list*, you will come back to it later in *Pathways* as you learn more about your behavior patterns and cycles. It may help you to think about this assignment if you draw on a separate piece of paper a picture or sketch of different sizes of barrels or crates. Label each barrel with the name of a problem you're having now or have had in the past. Some offenders draw their problems as barrels of dynamite or gasoline. Don't worry about being artistic.

Problems

1.

2.

3.

4.

5.

6.

7.

8.

9.

10.

[If you think of more, use the space at the bottom of the page.]

Goals

1.

2.

3.

4.

5.

6.

7.

8.

9.

10.

[If you think of more, use the space below.]

CHAPTER THREE

DISCLOSING: HOW DO I EXPLAIN WHAT I'VE DONE?

Since you're reading this book, you've either told someone about your harmful sexual activity or been caught. Someone besides the person you abused knows at least some of what you did. But now is the time to get honest about what you did and how you felt before, during, and after your offense. You need to tell your treatment group and your counselor, since they've made a commitment to support you in your treatment process. After that, you will have to decide who else you will tell about your sexual behavior, and what you will say.

You will be tempted to lie, avoid the truth, and leave out details when you talk about your sexual behavior to your group, your counselor, your parents or foster parents, your lawyer, the judge, and/or your probation or parole officer, among other people. You may also try to blame your behavior on other people or events. These urges are part of "denial," a stage that many offenders go through. The sooner you get through your initial stage of denial, the sooner your treatment can get underway. Treatment cannot really start until your counselor knows about all of your sexual behavior. If you lie to your counselor or leave out important details, he or she won't be able to give you the help you need and deserve. When you lie, you destroy any trust and respect you might have built up.

The answer to feeling tempted to lie is first, to make a commitment, a promise, to yourself that you will never lie to your counselor or your treatment group about your sexual behavior—or anything else. Your treatment program may have asked you to sign a written contract promising to tell the truth before starting treatment. If you signed the contract, make sure you live up to it.

Next, teach yourself to say, "I'm not ready to talk about that yet, can we come back to it later?" Talking about sexual matters is not easy, and talking about the details of a sexual offense is even harder. No matter how sincere you are, you will be tempted to lie about your sexual behavior! By teaching yourself to say you are not ready to talk about it, you are learning assertiveness skills, building trust by not lying, and starting the process of being honest about all parts of your life. **But if you use this statement as a wall to hide behind, it's just the same as lying.**

It takes a strong, intelligent, courageous person to face up to a problem like sexual offending. Anybody can avoid problems, hide the truth, run away, or blame somebody else. Many teenagers just like you have the guts and strength to face their mistakes, swallow their pride, and avoid lying during the disclosure process. If you are able to learn this now, before you have added to your mistakes by distorting the truth or denying your offenses, then you will be making good progress in treatment. Yes, this is treatment: admitting and understanding the whole problem is the only way treatment will work. If you hide the truth and try to show only the "good side" of you, then you will never really get the help you need and deserve.

Almost every sex offender initially denies some part of his/her sexual offenses. Denial serves some important purposes for sex offenders, since so many deny their offenses. Reasons why sex offenders deny their offenses include:

Why I Might Want To Deny My Sexual Offenses

— "I'm afraid my parents will kick me out."

— "But I'll get in so much trouble!

— "This is so embarrassing!"

— "I can't talk about—uh—you know—uh, sex."

— "If my boss finds out she'll fire me!"

— "None of my friends will talk to me if they know. They'll think I'm weird."

— "I'll have a record if I admit this—what if I want to go to college or join the army?"

— "People will look down on me."

— "But my lawyer said not to—it'll hurt my court case."

— "I won't be able to look at myself in the mirror."

— "People will call me a pervert."

— "If the others in detention find out, they'll beat me up."

— "I don't have to tell—my folks believe me when I say it never happened."

Assignment #3-A: Denial. Now list your reasons for wanting to deny the full extent of your sexual behavior. Some of your reasons may be the same as the ones listed above, but think of as many other reasons as possible that apply to you:

_____

_____

_____

_____

_____

_____

_____

_____

_____

_____

If you need more space, use a separate piece of paper.

While there are many reasons for denying sexual offenses, there are better reasons for telling the whole truth about your sexual behavior. Below are some reasons sex offenders decide to tell the whole truth about their sexual behavior:

Why I Want to Tell the Truth About My Sexual Behavior

— "What a relief!"

— "People aren't treating me weird since I told."

— "The court sees that at least I'm trying."

— "I don't have to keep this weird secret any more."

— "If I tell now, I can get some help."

— "My folks deserve the truth—a lie would only hurt them even more."

— "If I tell the truth, I can get into the program."

— "Maybe people will start trusting me."

— "This is really hard, but it'll make me stronger."

— "The people I abused shouldn't have to fight to get help—if I tell, they'll be believed."

— "I feel like here, in the group, it's okay to tell."

— "I want somebody to believe me."

— "I need help."

— "I'm scared they'll catch me in a lie later."

— "I want to stop feeling weird."

— "I want help dealing with my folks, because they hate me."

Assignment #3-B: Truth. Now list your reasons for telling the whole truth about your sexual behavior. It is okay to use some of the reasons listed above as long as they apply to you. Think of as many reasons as possible:

_____

_____

_____

_____

_____

_____

_____

_____

_____

_____

_____

If you need more space, use a separate piece of paper.

Now compare your "denial" list with your "truth" list. If your denial list is longer than your truth list, you probably won't be able to tell the whole truth about your sexual behavior right now. You will need to work with your counselor and treatment group to eliminate some of the reasons on your denial list and add some reasons to your truth list.

Sometimes it helps to think of denial as a series of stages or roadblocks you go through. Below are three stages of denial:

Stage 1:   Denial of the event ("I wasn't there, she is lying, it was someone else, nothing happened, I'm being framed").

Stage 2:   Denial of responsibility ("I was drunk, I didn't know what I was doing, she wanted it, I was just going along with my friends").

Stage 3:   Denial of the continuing problem ("Now that I know it's wrong it won't happen again, it's in my past, I'm cured, it was a one-time thing").

To get over your denial you must admit that you committed your offenses, that it was a choice you made, and that you will be tempted to offend again even after treatment. If you can make it to this point you will be well on your way toward beginning the treatment process.

"Denial" is one type of "thinking error"—a mistaken belief that influences your behavior. Thinking errors are the little messages running through the back of your mind that make it seem okay to commit your offenses. Any time you make excuses for your offense, blame someone else, or suggest that what you did wasn't wrong, you're using a thinking error.[1]

THINKING ERRORS

Like most sex offenders, you probably use different thinking errors that contribute to your sexual offending. A thinking error is "a thought or statement which minimizes, rationalizes, justifies, excuses, or denies the true extent of a problem, feeling, or behavior." Words such as "only," "just," "never," "always," or "but" are clues that you may be using a thinking error. Below is a list of common thinking errors developed by sexual offenders based on actual statements they made during disclosure and/or treatment:

But it wasn't my fault!	But I didn't hurt her.
It was never planned.	She wanted it.
I didn't mean to do it!	I only fondled him.
I just wanted to experiment.	I wasn't thinking at the time.
I only did it once.	I only had intercourse once.
I almost penetrated.	I was just playing around.
I only touched her.	I didn't penetrate.
My victim didn't cry.	It wasn't very violent.
It was an accident.	It just happened.
The same thing happened to me.	I was set up.

---

[1]"Thinking errors" were first described by Samuel Yochelson & Stanton Samenow (1976-77). *The Criminal Personality*, Vol. I & II. Dunmore, PA: Jason Aronson, Inc.

I tried not to threaten him.

It won't happen again.

I was only joking.

She didn't say no.

Maybe I did something like that.

I used some force.

I don't know.

I just wanted to feel good.

These are the kinds of thinking errors you use to prevent yourself from making a full, open, and honest disclosure of your sexual offenses. You use thinking errors to ignore people's feelings and your own responsibility. Thinking errors help you pretend that what you do doesn't matter, doesn't hurt anybody, or that you have a right to do it no matter who gets hurt. To stay offense-free in the future, you will have to look at and change *all* of your thinking errors.

Assignment #3-C: My Thinking Errors. Write down all the thinking errors you have used since you started your offending. Include your thoughts that helped you justify or excuse your offending behavior. Be specific: for example, "I told myself she is too young to tell anybody," "I thought I would just do it once," or "I saw my dad do it so I thought it was okay."

_____

_____

_____

_____

_____

_____

_____

_____

_____

_____

_____

If you need more space, use a separate piece of paper.

When you are asked to tell something about your sexual offenses, you might think, "I can handle this on my own, nobody really needs to know." But you'd be seriously wrong about that. It's another thinking error, a stage of denial. Almost every sex offender says this at some time or another, but unfortunately, too many continue their offending patterns. Consider these comments from Richard, an adult sex offender who started offending as a teenager, and only recently began treatment:

> As a 42-year-old sex offender, finally in treatment, I can only say why didn't I put myself in treatment 30 years and 300-plus victims ago? Treatment for me means my one last gasp to be a man instead of a monster. If you are a teenager and reading this, look in a mirror and check your heart. Are you being honest with yourself? Do you need help? Do you like what you see and feel? If not, or even if you are confused and you are a sex offender of any kind, do yourself and those who love and care for you a big favor—get into treatment. Don't let your sexual problems and hang-ups rule your life. Reach out and get some help now

while you're young and most of your life can be put to good use. Please don't be like me and years from now look back on all kinds of heartache and victims—having to cry, wishing you could go back...you can't. But you can start now. Unlike me, you have a chance to change early in life and save yourself a lot of embarrassment, heartaches, and to have a victim-free life from this, the first day of your accountability. Good luck!

Or listen to what Lewis, another adult sex offender, has to say:

I cannot count the times I have said, "I can handle this, I don't need help and besides, who would I talk to?" I started early in life and was always sexually active before others my age. I played games as innocent as house, doctor, and others that I could throw a small twist in—sexual contact. I found as many victims as I could during that time because somehow I knew I could not be punished back then. I carried the burden of being a sexual offender for many, many years. As I became a teenager I found many ways to release my sexual frustrations. I kept my offending to myself so my family and friends were in a state of shock when I was finally caught 28 years later. I have spent 9 years of my life in prison and I have found many others like myself who were unable or unwilling to get any kind of treatment. I am finally in treatment now, and it is a part of my life that gives me hope that I will not reoffend again. In short, accept one fact—you are an offender. Now learn to live a life that is healthy and doesn't hurt others. Good luck!

Complete Disclosure

Now it's your turn! Complete disclosure means telling someone else about all of your problem sexual behaviors. It's the difference between "being caught" and "being honest," and it is never an easy or comfortable task. The third assignment for this chapter is a fill-in-the-blanks exercise to help you begin to sort out the details of all of your sexual behavior. **Only write down things that are absolutely true.** If you have not been caught for all of your offenses, it is okay to use only your victims' first names. For now, the most important thing is for you to be honest with yourself, your counselor, and/or your treatment group about the full extent of your sexual behavior.

To get the help you really need, you have to be honest about all of your sexual behavior. Because you could be prosecuted for any offenses officials are not yet aware of, you may list only the *first* name and age of your victims. Reporting undisclosed victims is considered a positive treatment step; it means you are making progress and are beginning to show that you care about other people. The important thing is for you to begin opening up and talking to your counselor, treatment group, parents, foster parents, or guardian about your sexually abusive behavior.

Assignment #3-D: Who I Hurt. Fill out the list below with each of your victim's names, your relationship with each victim, your victims' ages and your age when you started the abuse. Include all of your victims, not just ones you got caught for.

Victim's Name	Relationship	Victim's Age	My Age

If you need more space, use a separate piece of paper.

Below is a list describing different sexual behaviors. Some, but not all, are illegal. Whether or not they are illegal, it is *wrong* for *anyone* to use their power, age, or knowledge to force, bribe, trick, or pressure anyone into sexual contact, especially when they are smaller, weaker, or less capable.

Vaginal Penetration: Putting your penis, finger, or other object in a female's vagina. It is penetration even if your penis, finger, or object did not go all the way in—any attempt qualifies as penetration.

Anal Penetration: Putting your penis, finger, or other object in the anus (bottom) of another person.

Oral Intercourse or Oral Sexual Contact: Putting your mouth (lips, tongue) on the genital or anal area of another person, or having them do it to you.

Fellatio: Oral contact with a male's penis.

Cunnilingus: Oral contact with a female's vagina or clitoris.

Fondling: Touching a person's private parts (breasts, genitals, anus, or other body part) with your hands. Make sure you specify whether it was on top of or underneath the victim's clothes.

Masturbation: Rubbing the penis, clitoris, or vagina of your victim, or having your victim rub your penis, clitoris, or vagina.

Exposure: Showing your genitals (for girls, includes the breasts) to your victim (flashing or mooning), or masturbating in front of your victim.

Obscene Phone Calls: Calling someone on the telephone without telling who you are and saying sexual things without their consent.

Peeping or Voyeurism: Spying on or looking at someone when they are in a private place (such as their own home or a public bathroom stall).

Frottage: Rubbing up against or touching someone for your own sexual pleasure while you are in a public place. Usually, it is done in a crowded place (an elevator, bus, or subway, for example) so that the victim will think the contact is accidental.

Assignment #3-E: What I Did. In the space below, describe exactly what you did with each victim. Include the total number of incidents and a description of your sexual behaviors.

Victims' Names	Total # of Incidents	What I Did

If you need more space, use a separate piece of paper.

Assignment #3-F: *How I Did It.* In the space below, describe how you got each of the victims to go along with your sexual behavior. Include all bribes, threats, force, promises, stories, etc.

Victim's Name	How I Got Him/Her to Go Along With Me

If you need more space, use a separate piece of paper.

Assignment #3-G: *Victim Reactions.* Think about how each of your victims reacted to your sexual offenses. Describe exactly what each of your victims said or did while you were committing your offenses. Describe how their faces looked and how they held their bodies.

Victim's Name	Victim's Reaction During Offenses

If you need more space, use a separate piece of paper.

Assignment 3-H: *Victim's Feelings.* In the exercise above you described the behavioral reactions of your victims; this assignment is about their feelings. In the space below write how you think your victims actually felt during your offenses. Some possible examples are scared, confused, or loved.

Victim's Name	Feelings Before	Feelings During	Feelings After

If you need more space, use a separate piece of paper.

Assignment #3-I: Planning My Offenses. When sex offenders plan and think about their offenses ahead of time (as almost all sex offenders do), it's called "fantasizing." Sometimes offenders masturbate while fantasizing, sometimes they don't. In this assignment, list your plans for your offenses, including all thoughts of offending. When did you first think of offending? Where were you? How often did you have these thoughts before committing your offense: hourly? daily? weekly? monthly? How did your fantasies and planning thoughts change after your offense? Explain how far in advance you planned your offenses (if you have many offenses, estimate the best you can). **Keep this assignment!** It will help you when you work on understanding your cycle in Chapter Seven.

Victim's Name	My Planning

If you need more space, use a separate piece of paper.

Assignment #3-J: Getting Caught. Describe how you got caught for your offenses. Where were you and who was with you when you got caught? Who told? Who did they tell? Were the police called?

_____

_____

_____

_____

_____

_____

_____

_____

_____

If you need more space, use a separate piece of paper.

Assignment #3-K: Who Is Responsible? In the space below, list the name of each of your victims, how much responsibility for your sexual offenses against that victim belongs to you (0 means none, 100% means all), who else is responsible, and why.

Victim's Name	Who is Responsible		Why
	% Me	Who else	
_____	_____	_____	_____
_____	_____	_____	_____
_____	_____	_____	_____
_____	_____	_____	_____
_____	_____	_____	_____
_____	_____	_____	_____
_____	_____	_____	_____
_____	_____	_____	_____

If you need more space, use a separate piece of paper.

Assignment #3-L: Future Effects. List the names of each of your victims and what long-lasting effects your sexual offenses might have on them. Be specific.

Victim's Name	Effects of My Offense

_____

_____

_____

_____

_____

_____

If you need more space, use a separate piece of paper.

Assignment #3-M: Friends & Family. Explain how the important people in your life reacted when they found out about your sexual offenses. List what you think they were feeling as well as what they said or did.

Mother:_____

_____

_____

Father:_____

_____

_____

Brothers & Sisters:_____

_____

Other Relatives:_____

_____

Friends:_____

_____

_____

_____

If you need more space, use a separate piece of paper.

Assignment #3-N: Getting Honest. On a scale of 0 to 100%, how honest have you been with others about your sexual offenses (0 means you haven't been honest about anything, 100% means you've been completely honest about everything).

_____%

List all of the people to whom you have told the whole truth about all of your sexual offenses.

_____

_____

_____

_____

If you need more space, use a separate piece of paper.

List all of the people you have lied to in one way or another (avoiding the truth, not telling everything) about the full extent of your sexual behavior.

_____

_____

_____

_____

_____

_____

_____

_____

_____

_____

_____

If you need more space, use a separate piece of paper.

Assignment #3-O: Sexual History. Describe your first sexual experience you can remember.

_____

_____

_____

_____

_____

_____

_____

_____

_____

_____

If you need more space, use a separate piece of paper.

Assignment #3-P: Describe how and where you learned about sex when you were younger (include X-rated movies, magazines, books, school, watching others, telephone "sex lines," etc.).

_____

_____

_____

_____

_____

_____

_____

_____

_____

_____

_____

_____

_____

If you need more space, use a separate piece of paper.

Assignment #3-Q: Describe any and all sexual experiences you have had with anyone older than you, including incidents you consider mutual as well as nonconsenting.

_____

_____

_____

_____

_____

_____

_____

_____

_____

_____

If you need more space, use a separate piece of paper.

Assignment #3-R: List the sexual experience that you are most embarrassed and ashamed about (sex with animals, masturbating with women's underwear, molesting young children, etc.).

_____

_____

_____

_____

_____

_____

_____

If you need more space, use a separate piece of paper.

Assignment #3-S: Who else in your family has been in trouble for their sexual behavior (include grandparents, uncles, etc.)? Describe what they did that got them into trouble.

Person's First Name	What He/She Did

If you need more space, use a separate piece of paper.

Assignment #3-T: Who among your friends, relatives, or acquaintances do you personally know has been sexually abused (besides your victims)?

First Name	Relationship

If you need more space, use a separate piece of paper.

Assignment #3-U: List everybody you have ever had any sexual contact with (including all your victims). Start with your first contact and go in order through your most recent sexual encounter.

Name	My Age	His/Her Age	Sexual Activities

If you need more space, use a separate piece of paper.

Okay, you've finished for now. If you were able to answer all of the questions you did a great job! The answers you've given on these assignments will help you answer most of the hard questions that your counselor or treatment group will ask.

CHAPTER FOUR

LEARNING ABOUT VICTIMS

One of the most important goals of treatment is to learn how your sexual offenses have affected the lives of the people you abused. First, let's look at some of the common myths about victims of sexual abuse. A *myth* is a belief some people have that is not true. Here are some myths and truths about sexual abuse:

Myth #1: Children are only harmed when offenders use force to make them have sex with them.

Truth #1: Children can suffer lots of different kinds of harm, including fear, embarrassment, shame, guilt, and rejection by others. Sometimes physical pain goes away quickly, while emotional pain can stay a long time.

Myth #2: Children often lie by making up stories of sexual abuse.

Truth #2: Cases of children lying about sexual abuse are rare. Research has shown, however, that most sex offenders lie about their offenses and may try to blame their victims.

Myth #3: A sexual act is rape only if the person tries to fight back the entire time.

Truth #3: A sexual act is rape anytime a person has sex with another person without his/her consent. Many victims choose not to fight back because they are afraid of being hurt or because the offender is bigger or stronger or has threatened him or her in some way.

Myth #4: Very young children can decide for themselves about having sex.

Truth #4: Our society has established the age of 16 as the age of consent in most states and provinces. Very young children, especially, are easy to take advantage of and don't have enough experience or knowledge to make decisions about sexual relations.

Myth #5: If a child doesn't tell about having sex, then he/she liked it.

Truth #5: Children don't tell because of fear, embarrassment, shame, wanting to protect parents, or for many other reasons. Not telling does not mean that a child "liked" the abuse, or that a peer or adult "liked" being raped, spied on, or flashed.

Myth #6: Some people are so shy about asking for sex that they really want you to force sex on them.

Truth #6: Nobody wants to have sex forced on them, shy or not.

Myth #7: If someone stares at my private parts while I'm exposing them, it means the person likes it.

Truth #7: Sometimes people stare because they are surprised, shocked, afraid, confused, or embarrassed. It does not mean liking it.

Myth #8: Sexually hurting someone is okay in some situations.

Truth #8: Though horror movies may show such scenes, in real life, this behavior is *never* acceptable.

Myth #9: If I just look through the windows at somebody, it can't hurt them.

Truth #9: Seeing someone outside a window can be terrifying, and can cause a person to be afraid, worried, anxious, and concerned. This type of emotional violation can be a terrible experience.

Myth #10: Most sex offenses are caused by the victim acting sexy around the offender.

Truth #10: Sex offenses are caused only by offenders, and no one else. Sex offenders often try to place blame and responsibility on the people they abused.

Now that you are beginning to understand some of the myths and truths about sexual abuse, it is important that you develop some understanding of the thoughts and feelings your victims might be experiencing. Below is a list of feelings that victims of sexual and/or physical abuse commonly experience.

Feelings of Abuse Victims

1. Suspicious, unable to trust others

2. Afraid, unable to stand up for own opinion

3. Blames self for everything bad that happens

4. Feels guilty and ashamed even when there is no reason

5. Withdraws, doesn't want to spend time with others

6. Feels "different" from others

7. Feels hurt by others a lot of the time

8. Lonely, bored, and empty inside

9. Suicidal

10. Feels like a perfectionist, can't tolerate mistakes

11. Constantly feels sorry for self

12. Feels angry all the time

13. Closes off feelings, unable to tolerate emotional pain

14. Not caring about appearance

15. Feels out of control of life

16. Depressed and sad

17. Afraid of change

18. Feels trapped, like nobody understands

19. Feels stupid, less capable than others

20. Ashamed of sexual feelings

One way to learn about how victims feel is to think about some questions (below) they might want to ask you. They may not be able to ask these questions out loud because they're scared, shy, embarrassed, or for many other reasons. But one of the things you can do to begin helping your victim is to answer these questions for your victim and for yourself. Later in *Pathways* you will use this information to write letters to your victim(s).

Questions Victims of Sexual Abuse May Ask

1. Why did you do those things to me?

2. Why did you pick me, what did I do?

3. Will you ever do those things to me again?

4. Have you done that to anyone else?

5. Are you getting counseling now?

6. How has counseling helped you?

7. Do you still love me?

8. If you loved me, why did you do this to me?

9. How will I know if you are about to hurt me again?

10. Should I trust you any more?

11. What can I do to protect myself if I feel you're about to do those things to me?

12. How do you feel about my telling on you and you getting into trouble?

13. Did anybody else know what you were doing when this was happening?

14. What would have happened if you hadn't have been caught?

15. Are you going to come home?

16. How will things be different when you come home?

17. Will my friends be safe after you come home?

18. Who needs to know about what you did?

19. Who knows now about what you did?

20. Tell me about your counseling.

Add any others you have been asked or have heard about:

21. _____

22. _____

23. _____

The following exercise is designed to help you become more aware of what it is like to go through a sexual abuse experience. It starts with a relaxation exercise, then Donnie's little brother tells about when Donnie was abused. If you are not a good reader you may find it helpful to have your counselor read this exercise to you or to put it on tape and listen to it later.

How to Relax

First of all, find a seat in a comfortable chair, where nobody will disturb you for a few minutes. Take several deep breaths and let the air out of your lungs slowly.

Now, picture in your mind a beautiful mountain meadow in the springtime. There is a small lake nearby and a gentle breeze is blowing through the tall trees surrounding the meadow. The ground is covered with lush green clover, and wildflowers color the green ground with speckles of red, orange, purple, and yellow. The sky is clear and the air is crisp and fresh, with just a hint of evergreen needles in the air. Breathe deeply and imagine being in the meadow, gently seated in the clover, enjoying the peace and serenity of the meadow. No one can bother you there, you are safe and happy.

Donnie's Brother Remembers

Okay, you are now going to go back to when you were four years old. I want you to imagine living in a small house near the edge of town. Your mother works during the day because your dad left when you were younger. You have not yet started school, and you spend lots of time playing with your six-year-old brother, Donnie, and watching TV. Your favorite day of the week is Saturday when you and your brother get to watch cartoons all morning. You and Donnie live alone with your mother and since the house only has two bedrooms, you and your brother share one. Imagine what the room looks like, toys all over the floor and clothes hanging on the only chair in the room.

Your mom works for an insurance company and sometimes has to work late into the evening. Usually when she needs to work late she calls a neighbor girl, Jenny, who comes over and fixes sandwiches and stays to put you and Donnie to bed. On this day, though, Jenny has other plans and your mom has to find another babysitter. She calls another neighbor, Billy, and asks him to babysit. He has babysat a few times before and everything was okay. Billy sometimes played with the little kids in the neighborhood and even though he was sometimes mean, he was always nice to you and Donnie.

On this night, Billy comes over and you all have some cereal and milk, then you all watch TV. At seven o'clock Billy sends you to bed, which you don't like because normally you and Donnie go to bed at the same time. As you get ready for bed you realize that you really miss your mom and you wish she was there to say good night to you.

A few minutes after getting into your bed you remember that you haven't used the bathroom so you get up and go to the door of your room. You hear your brother's voice asking Billy what he is doing. You then hear Billy saying, "It's okay Donnie—I'll let you make popcorn if you play the game." Since you are a little worried and a little curious you quietly open the door and peek out into the TV room. Through the crack in the door you see Billy sitting next to Donnie with his arm on Donnie's leg. This seems kind of strange to you so you open the door a few inches more, and then you open it all the way and walk into the room toward the bathroom. When Billy sees you he gets really mad and tells you to go back and get into bed. You look at Billy and realize that Donnie looks tiny compared to him. He sounds really mean right now so you quickly go back to your own room. After closing the door, you stand there to listen if Billy is coming to check on you. You can feel your heart pounding, hoping that nothing happens. He doesn't come and you hear Donnie saying in the living room, "I don't want to play, Billy!"

A few minutes later, you hear him yell, "I'm going to tell my mommy!" You then hear Billy saying, "Be quiet, just do it." When you don't hear anything else you again quietly open the door and peek out. What you see really confuses you.

Billy is holding Donnie's head down between his legs and moving it up and down. Donnie seems to be crying, but you can't really tell for sure. You open the door a little more to see better. Billy raises his head and sees you looking out and yells, "Shut that door or I'll kick your ass!" You quickly close the door and go lie down in your bed holding on tightly to your covers. You lie on your bed clenching your fists, thinking to yourself that you wish your mom was home and that Billy had never come over.

A while later Donnie comes into the room and you notice he has tears in his eyes. You ask, "What happened Donnie, did Billy hurt you?" Donnie says, "Not exactly," and then tells you he's not supposed to talk about it. You go to sleep wondering what happened in the living room, and wondering if Billy would ever do the same thing to you.

Assignment #4-A: Donnie's Feelings. List all of the feelings you think Donnie would have had during the incident.

_____

_____

_____

_____

_____

_____

_____

_____

_____

_____

_____

_____

_____

_____

_____

If you need more space, use a separate piece of paper.

Assignment #4-B: My Feelings. List all of the feelings you think you would have had if you just experienced this situation.

_____

_____

_____

_____

_____

_____

_____

_____

_____

_____

_____

_____

_____

_____

_____

If you need more space, use a separate piece of paper.

Assignment #4-C: *My Gut Reactions.* Describe your gut-level reaction to reading or listening to this story.

_____

_____

_____

_____

_____

_____

_____

_____

_____

_____

_____

_____

_____

_____

_____

_____

_____

If you need more space, use a separate piece of paper.

Assignment #4-D: *Similar Situations*. Describe any similar situation you have had where you might have experienced similar feelings.

_____

_____

_____

_____

_____

_____

_____

_____

_____

_____

_____

_____

_____

_____

_____

_____

_____

_____

_____

_____

_____

_____

_____

_____

_____

_____

_____

_____

_____

_____

_____

_____

_____

If you need more space, use a separate piece of paper.

LEARNING ABOUT BOUNDARIES

Sexual abuse victims have had their boundaries broken, shattered, ignored, violated, or simply not respected. A boundary is an imaginary wall or line that keeps us feeling safe, comfortable, and protected. Persons with sexual behavior problems often don't understand or respect the boundaries of other people. They are so *preoccupied* with their own urges and desires, that they don't care about the feelings or belongings of other people. In treatment, it is very important that you learn to understand and respect the boundaries of other people, as well as to protect and stand up for your own boundaries. You will use these skills for the rest of your life.

A boundary can be a lot of different things. A boundary can be anything you want to keep private, special or personal. A boundary can be a thing, a place, a thought or a feeling. Some examples of boundaries are your body, your personal feelings, your room, your notebook, your treatment homework, your diary, or your past experiences. Let's start with obvious boundaries. For most people, your belongings represent boundaries. Take a favorite thing like a CD player for example. It belongs to you and you probably don't want other people taking it. This is a boundary for you. Another example is your body. While you might not mind someone shaking your hand, you might not want someone coming up and touching your stomach or your bottom. That is your boundary. Another example might be your experience as a victim of sexual abuse. It would be a violation of *your boundaries* for someone else to tell about what happened to you. That is private.

You have violated someone else's boundaries. It is okay to talk about your experiences as a sex offender, but it is not okay to tell others about the identity of the person you abused without his or her permission. This shows the beginnings of respect for someone else's boundaries. This rule does not apply when you talk to your counselor or treatment group about your offending behavior. Not revealing the identities of the people you abused to your counselor is keeping a dangerous secret and may prevent them from being offered the help they need to heal.

Assignment #4-E: What are some physical boundaries that help you feel safe, respected, and secure? (For example, your body, your possessions, your room, your locker, your gym bag, etc.).

1._____

2._____

3._____

4._____

5._____

Assignment #4-F: What are some emotional boundaries that you would like respected in your life? Include things you might feel sensitive or insecure about, like health concerns, sex life, weight, height, life experiences, etc. Think of some examples not on this list and be as detailed as you can:

1._____

2._____

3._____

4._____

5._____

As you go through *Pathways*, you will be asked to demonstrate that you can respect the boundaries of other people. This is one of the best ways you can show that treatment is helping you. On the other hand, one of the best ways to show that treatment is not helping you is to disrespect the boundaries of other people. To become a member of the sexual abuse prevention team, you must show that you are not *self-centered*, and that you respect other people. If you shoplift or steal things from other people, then you are violating boundaries and giving in to self-centered behavior. In that respect, when you steal or otherwise violate people's boundaries, you are doing something that is very much like committing a new sex offense.

Assignment #4-G: Now, list some ways that you have violated the boundaries of other people during the past year (include problem sexual behavior, unwanted touching, stealing, gossiping, disrespecting a person's feelings, verbal put-downs, trespassing, etc): Be very specific about what you have done.

1._____

2._____

3._____

4._____

5._____

CHAPTER FIVE

WHY DID I DO IT?

UNDERSTANDING HOW I COMMITTED MY SEXUAL OFFENSES

Sexual offenses do not just "happen." A series of events must occur before you commit a sexual offense. These events are called "preconditions" ("pre" means "before").[1] These conditions must exist *before* you commit a sexual offense. For each precondition to exist, you had to have broken through or gotten over some barrier or wall that ordinarily prevents people from committing sexual offenses. *Pathways* is about learning how to stop going over or through the walls and barriers. In this chapter you will learn about your *preconditions* for abuse and how to build up the barriers to prevent yourself from offending again.

Look at the chart below. Imagine yourself as the person on the left, who could only offend against the person on the right by climbing over or breaking through the barriers that separate you. If you could not get over the walls, you would not reach the victim. The next section explains the four preconditions: (1) motivation, (2) internal barriers, (3) external barriers, and (4) the victim's resistance.

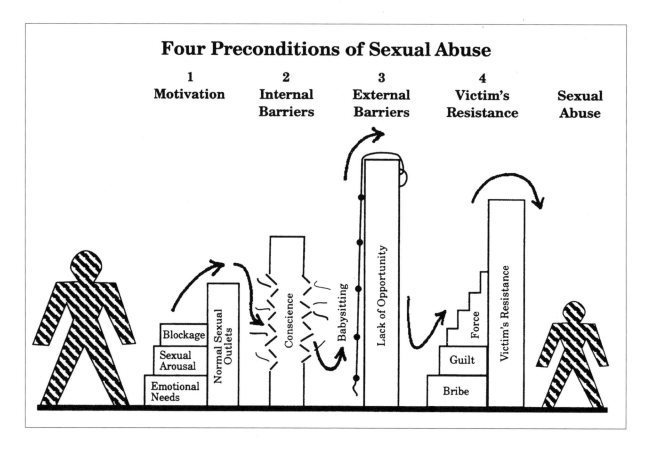

Four Preconditions of Sexual Abuse

1 Motivation | 2 Internal Barriers | 3 External Barriers | 4 Victim's Resistance | Sexual Abuse

Blockage, Sexual Arousal, Emotional Needs — Normal Sexual Outlets — Conscience — Babysitting — Lack of Opportunity — Bribe, Guilt — Force — Victim's Resistance

---

[1]This theory is called "Four Preconditions: A Model." See Finkelhor, D. (1984) *Child Sexual Abuse: New Theory & Research* (pp. 53-68). New York: Free Press.

1. **Motivation.** The first precondition was that you *wanted* to molest the child or rape the other person if you were going to go to all the trouble of climbing the walls between you. *Motivation*, in this case, means what makes you *want* to offend. With most sexual offenders, the motivation is your sexual urge, fantasy, or thought. But not every thought leads to an offense—you had to overcome other barriers that also stand in the way of your offending.

   You may have developed the motivation to offend sexually in any of several different ways: because of your *emotional needs*, by your experiences of *sexual arousal*, or by the *blockage* of your normal sexual expression.

   Emotional needs. You may have a need for power and control, or simply relate better socially with children. You may be emotionally "young" or lonely and don't feel comfortable with peers, people your own age. Maybe you feel insecure about yourself or are afraid of rejection. You might feel angry and take that anger out on others. Any of these factors could contribute to your developing the motivation to offend sexually.

   Sexual arousal. You might have developed a motivation to offend because you experience sexual urges toward children. One way that might have happened is if you were molested as a young child, told no one, and the person who molested you was never caught. An experience like that might have taught you that sex with children is safe. Or you might have tried to stop feeling powerless and helpless about having been molested by putting yourself in the role of the abuser. Or you may have had an early sexual experience that was arousing and exciting, and you want to recreate that experience of satisfaction and reward by having sexual contact with children. It is also possible that pornography played a role in forming your early sexual interest.

   Blockage. Blockage happened when you had normal sexual urges, but something stood in the way of your being able to express them normally. For instance, if you were brought up to believe that masturbating is immoral or wrong, the only way to meet your sexual needs would be with a partner. You might be too shy or insecure to risk getting involved with a person the same age as you. It may feel emotionally much safer to have a relationship with a child who is easy to impress. Maybe you don't have good social skills, you feel awkward in relationships with peers, or you were never taught good personal hygiene; any of these things could have played a part in blocking you from expressing your sexual feelings normally with peers.

2. **Internal Barriers.** Once you had the motivation, you convinced yourself that you *should* commit the offense. You had to do three things: get past your fear of getting caught, decide that the victim's feelings don't matter, and ignore the fact that you know it is wrong. In other words, your desire to offend was stronger than your conscience telling you that you shouldn't do it. These *internal barriers* are fairly strong in other teenagers; in sexual offenders they are usually very weak.

   All people talk to themselves inside their own minds, making comments and observations about the world around them, how they feel, and what they think. Certain kinds of mistaken self-talk break down your *internal barriers* against offending. You may have told yourself that you were so smooth, so cool, and so smart that you'd never get caught. You might have told yourself that you were so angry, you had a right to take out your anger on anybody who was available by forcing them to have sex. If you were under stress (when everything seemed to be going wrong) or depressed, you might have told yourself that it didn't matter what you did, or you didn't care what happened. You might not have understood how harmful sexual abuse is to those who are victimized. If you grew up in a family with other sexual offenders and victims, you may not have learned what normal sexual boundaries are in a healthy family. These are all examples of ways you probably broke down your internal barriers against offending.

3. **External Barriers.** The third precondition came into play after you *wanted* to offend and *decided* you were going to do it. Then you had to find a *way* to do it. You had to get the victim alone and make sure no one was watching for a long enough time for you to commit your offense. *External barriers* are very important—you can have the urge and decide to do it, but you can't offend unless you find access to the victim. Building up external barriers is a big part of the treatment process in *Pathways,* and one over which you have a lot of control.

You had choices to make in order to get access to the person you abused. You volunteered or somebody asked you to babysit, and you said yes. You went to the playground where the little kids play. You told your mom you'd look after your sister while she went shopping. Your kid brother asked to go on the hike with you, and you said yes. You agreed because you knew it would give you the time and the opportunity to make sexual contact with the person you abused. A majority of teenage sex offenders commit their sexual offenses while babysitting, when they have their victims alone and they are in charge. By making the choice not to babysit, you can shut off one of your easiest opportunities and strongest temptations to offend.

For sex offenders like you, it's a lot harder to reoffend when you stay away from possible victims. This is one of the simplest parts of treatment, but many offenders resist this step. It's almost as if they want to "prove" they're "cured" by subjecting themselves to the temptation to offend. But if you want to maintain yourself as a member of the sexual offender safety and prevention team, you have to choose to walk away from temptation.

It's a little like kicking an addiction. If you quit smoking but still hung around the cigarette machine, you'd wind up smoking again. But if you kept right on walking and stayed out of smoking rooms, it would help you stick to your program. Or a driver who is about to lose his/her license for speeding might decide to take the bus to avoid giving himself/herself the opportunity to speed. Recovering alcoholics avoid bars for the same reason.

Building up your external barriers is part of "relapse prevention." It takes planning and thinking ahead to change your life so that you will have fewer opportunities to reoffend. In Chapter Nine you will learn more about planning how to prevent yourself from reoffending.

4. **Victim's Resistance.** Finally, once you got past the external barriers, you had to overcome the victim's resistance. You might have given the victim candy, threatened the victim, made him or her feel sorry for you, or forced the victim to do what you wanted. Many teenage sex offenders pick very young, very quiet, or very shy children as victims because it is so easy to overcome their resistance and they are less likely to tell. About 40 percent of the victims of teenage offenders are 4 years old or younger. There is no way a 3- or 4-year-old can make his/her resistance to being abused count against the knowledge and power of a teenager.

The Four Preconditions chart is the blueprint for how you commit your sexual offenses. It is also a blueprint for your treatment, since you can learn to build up any of the four walls or barriers to prevent further offenses. In Pathways, one of the goals of treatment is to help you build up all four barriers, with the hope that at least one will become high enough to prevent you from committing a reoffense.

Now it is time for you to look at your own offending history. The following assignment is designed to help you figure out for yourself how you got past each of the four walls.

Assignment #5: How I Set Up My Four Preconditions for Sexual Abuse. In each of the next four assignments, you will give examples of how you set up each of the four preconditions for sexual abuse in order to commit your offenses. Use your victim's first name and be as specific as possible.

Assignment #5-A: Motivation to Sexually Abuse. Describe what you think gave you the idea and the interest in having sexual contact with the person(s) you abused. Describe to what extent your motivation to sexually offend continues to be a problem for you.

_____

_____

_____

_____

_____

_____

_____

_____

_____

_____

_____

If you need more space, use a separate piece of paper.

Assignment #5-B: Internal Barriers. After you realized you were interested in having sexual contact with the person(s) you abused, how did you convince yourself to do it? Describe your self-talk. What did you say to yourself that made it seem all right to offend?

_____

_____

_____

_____

_____

_____

_____

_____

_____

_____

_____

_____

_____

_____

_____

_____

_____

_____

_____

If you need more space, use a separate piece of paper.

Assignment #5-C: External Barriers. Once you convinced yourself it was all right to have sex with the person(s) you abused, how did it become a possibility? Describe how you went about finding the right time and place for it to happen. List all the external barriers (what could have stopped you) which were absent during your offenses.

_____

_____

_____

_____

_____

_____

_____

_____

_____

_____

_____

_____

_____

_____

_____

_____

If you need more space, use a separate piece of paper.

Assignment #5-D: Victim's Resistance. How did you overcome any resistance by the people you abused? List all coercive games, promises, threats, bribes, etc. Why did you pick this particular victim—what made him/her particularly easy or attractive to you as a victim?

_____

_____

_____

_____

_____

_____

_____

_____

_____

_____

_____

_____

_____

_____

_____

_____

_____

_____

_____

_____

_____

_____

_____

_____

_____

_____

If you need more space, use a separate piece of paper.

Now you are on your way toward understanding how you commit your offenses. In the next two chapters you'll learn more about how you commit your offenses, which will help you learn how to stop. You will also put together a plan to build up all four barriers to reoffending.

CHAPTER SIX

IDENTIFYING MY GROOMING AND MAINTENANCE BEHAVIORS

In order to avoid the blame and responsibility that go along with planning offenses ahead of time, most sex offenders want to believe their offenses "just happened." What they don't realize, however, is that offenders who do not pre-plan their offenses are the most dangerous. The out-of-control offender who can offend at a moment's notice with no warning, pre-planning, or pre-thought is the highest risk to others. If you think about your offenses ahead of time, you can learn ways of changing and interrupting your thinking to avoid reoffending. This chapter will help you identify and understand how you set up and prepare the people you abused for sexual contact (known as "grooming"), as well as how your day-to-day behavior supports further offending. By understanding and changing this behavior, you will start to build up your barriers to reoffending.

GROOMING BEHAVIORS

Grooming is like flirting, except that when you're grooming someone, you already know that you intend to have sex with that victim. For example, not every video-game player is a sex offender; but some sex offenders use such games to gain their victims' trust and interest. In these cases, playing video games is part of the grooming process. The following list (developed by a group of adolescent sexual offenders who were involved in peer-group treatment) includes examples of the types of activities teenage sex offenders use to groom their victims.

1. I would make up games that would interest him or her.

2. I would constantly be with them and find out what they'd be willing to do with me.

3. I acted like I didn't want them to see the sexual book I was reading. That got them interested.

4. I would get them into horseplay and playful wrestling.

5. I would take off their clothes during horseplay.

6. We would play Nintendo or other computer games together.

7. I would sleep in the same room with her and climb on top of her body and act like I was asleep.

8. I would play house with him.

9. I would buy them toys and candy.

10. I would invite them to sleep with me and I would be nude before they came into the room.

11. I would increase physical contact; I would have the kids I abused sitting on my lap and would give them piggy-back rides.

12. I would appear to be hugging the person I abused, but I was having sexual thoughts.

13. I started by pretending to be interested in children's toys.

14. I would be kind to them and then become more than a friend.

15. I would always spend my free time with the people I abused so I could catch on to the things they liked to do.

16. I would show them Playboy and Playgirl magazines.

17. If he would do sexual things with me, I would promise to protect him from other kids who would beat him up.

Assignment #6-A: Grooming. List all the things that you did to prepare or set up your victim for sexual contact. This list will be your own personal summary of your grooming behavior.

1._____

2._____

3._____

4._____

5._____

6._____

7._____

If you need more space, use a separate piece of paper.

This list of your grooming behaviors will help you as you develop your offense prevention plan in Chapter Nine. ***All of your grooming behaviors are warning signs that you are in your offense pattern and are at high risk of further sexual offenses.*** To avoid reoffending, you have to choose every day not to put yourself in any of the situations on your list.

MAINTENANCE BEHAVIORS

Your day-to-day behavior contributes to your choice to offend sexually. Your sexual behavior is controlled by your brain. A *maintenance behavior* is any behavior that feeds into your sexual problem and maintains your abusive sexual behaviors. Maintenance behaviors are not targeted toward any one person. They are the things you do that keep you thinking about offending, enable you to keep hurting other people, and keep you from feeling good and successful about yourself. They support and reinforce sexual offending and tend to increase your risk to offend.

The following list of maintenance behaviors was developed by adolescent sexual offenders undergoing specialized treatment.

1. Talking about sexual things

2. Making sexual gestures with my body

3. Writing sexual things and violent things

4. Having "bad" sexual fantasies

5. Making fun of a person's body

6. Giving up or falling back in treatment

7. Sex talk in letters

8. Calling people sexual names

9. Touching people in nonsexual ways when they don't want to be touched

10. Trying to get my own way

11. Acting bossy

12. Reading books with negative talk about sex (like ones which make it sound like rape is an okay thing)

13. Watching a movie that has a rape scene, or talks about sex in a bad way

14. Following people around

15. Going on a "power trip," which means bossing people around

16. Masturbating while thinking about offending

17. Blaming other people for my own problems or behavior

18. Putting things off, not following through on responsibilities

19. Seeking negative attention

20. Lying about my day-to-day behavior

21. Using "thinking errors"

22. Using drugs and alcohol

23. Putting other people down

24. Acting selfish, not caring about others

Assignment #6-B: Maintenance Behaviors. Now think about your own day-to-day behavior and make up a list of all of your maintenance behaviors. If you have trouble, remember to consult with your counselor or parents.

1._____

2._____

3._____

4._____

5._____

6._____

7._____

8._____

If you need more space, use a separate piece of paper.

The maintenance behaviors you have listed will become a part of your Offense Prevention Plan in Chapter Nine. As you will see in Chapter Seven, a big part of your treatment involves learning about your cycles of maintenance behaviors and how you can change the behaviors that lead to offending. For your treatment program to be successful, you will need to find a way to control or eliminate these maintenance behaviors. The following assignment will help you begin to build up your reoffense barriers by changing your grooming and maintenance behaviors.

Assignment 6-C: Building up My Barriers. Take another look at your list of grooming and maintenance behaviors. On the following diagram list changes you can make that will help you build up your barriers to reoffending. **Start at the bottom—the more changes you can list the higher the barrier will be.**

I won't touch anyone without their consent.

Thinking about others first, showing I care.

CHAPTER SEVEN

UNDERSTANDING MY PRE-OFFENSE PATTERN AND MY OFFENSE AND MAINTENANCE CYCLES

In Chapter Five you learned about the Four Preconditions to Sexual Abuse—the effort you had to go to and the choices you had to make to overcome the barriers to committing your sexual offense. Another way to think about how you get to the point of committing a sexual offense is in a cycle. A *cycle* is a repeating pattern of thoughts and feelings, events, and behaviors that produce the same result over and over again. Sexual offenses are made up of two parts: your *pre-offense pattern* and your *offense cycle*.

Kim is having nightmares about when she was little and being sexually abused by her father. She is keeping those scared, shaky feelings to herself. She is also beginning puberty and having new and confusing sexual feelings. She feels bored and lonely, and her parents often ask her to babysit her younger brother. This is her pre-offense pattern.

Your *pre-offense pattern* is the pattern of thoughts and feelings, events, and activities that happens *before* you start thinking about committing your particular sexual offense as a way to cope with them. For example, Mark is failing in school, having problems getting along with his mom, and feels bored a lot of the time. This is *his* pre-offense pattern.

When you actually start thinking about the sexual contact, having fantasies, planning, looking for ways to spend time with the victim (or figuring out which house has good windows to peep into, or when you can make phone calls, and so on), then you are in your *offense cycle*. Mark enters his offense cycle when he tries to push the bad feelings to the back of his mind by thinking about how powerful he feels when he makes his six-year-old brother David masturbate him. Kim enters into her offense cycle when she starts to experience sexual thoughts towards her brother.

These two parts of your sexual offense are connected by a bridge of mistaken self-talk—just like two banks of a river are connected by a bridge. You can't move from your pre-offense pattern into your offense cycle without the bridge created by your mistaken self-talk—just like you can't walk from one side of a river to the other without a bridge.

In Chapter Five you learned that mistaken self-talk is what you tell yourself in order to break down your internal barriers to offending. Mistaken self-talk is usually made up of *thinking errors* like the ones you learned about in Chapter Three. They help you deny, justify, or minimize your responsibility for committing a sexual offense. We saw in Chapter Five that building up the barriers to offending is one way of preventing yourself from offending again. Changing your self-talk by getting rid of your *thinking errors* and learning responsible ways to think is a necessary step in this process.

MY PRE-OFFENSE PATTERN WORKSHEET

This worksheet helps you explore all of the factors in your life that contributed to your choosing to act out sexually. In the space below list all of the events, behaviors, and feelings that were occurring in your life just before your offenses began.

Assignment #7-A: Events in My Life. Examples: Problems in school; parents' divorce, major illness, or death; rejection by friends; sexual or physical abuse by another person; alcoholic parent, stepparent, or other caretaker; and so on.

_____

_____

_____

_____

_____

_____

_____

_____

_____

_____

_____

_____

_____

_____

_____

_____

If you need more space, use a separate piece of paper.

Assignment #7-B: My Behaviors. Examples: Fighting, using drugs, spending lots of time alone, avoiding others, running away from home, arguing with parents, skipping school, shoplifting, joyriding, etc.

_____

_____

_____

_____

_____

_____

_____

_____

_____

_____

_____

_____

_____

_____

If you need more space, use a separate piece of paper.

Assignment #7-C: My Feelings. Examples: Angry, alone, unloved, insecure, sad, cold, curious, bored, shy, afraid, nervous, worthless, hopeless, tense, happy, horny, etc.

_____

_____

_____

_____

_____

_____

_____

_____

_____

_____

_____

_____

_____

_____

If you need more space, use a separate piece of paper.

Mapping My Pre-offense Pattern

To help you understand your offending pattern, you can make a timeline, like a road map through time, of your offenses.

Assignment #7-D: Timelines. On the next page are some timelines. For each victim you had, write his or her first name and age below the month when you started having sexual contact. Then draw a dotted line until you reach the month when you stopped that particular offense, and make an x. Start with the earliest offense you can remember, fill in what year it happened at the top of the timeline, then start listing. If you molested the same victim in more than one year, list his or her name again on the second timeline, and the third, if necessary. Make as many more timelines as you need.

Just below where you've listed the names the people you abused and drawn the lines, list the *life events* from the last exercise below the name of the month when they happened. For an example of how to make your timeline, look at the one made by Tony, a 15-year-old offender in a treatment group. If you're having trouble, ask your group leader for help.

When you're done, you'll be able to see if there might be a relationship between what was happening in your life and when you started to offend. The events did not *cause* you to offend—lots of teenagers go through hard times just like yours and don't commit sexual offenses. But the way you *responded* to some of these events pointed you in the direction of a sexual offense, gave you the opportunity to offend, or played some other role in your offense pattern.

Tony's Timeline

19<u>96</u>

| Jan. | Feb. | Mar. | Apr. | May | Jun. | Jul. | Aug. | Sep. | Oct. | Nov. | Dec. |

Victims: Mary (age 4) . . . . .X (stopped Oct.)
Scott (age 6) . . . . . . .X (stopped Aug.)

Events: Mom started dating
new boyfriend   Arrested
                                                                 (Nov.)

Suspended   Started
from school   Summer job X

Name:

19___

| Jan. | Feb. | Mar. | Apr. | May | Jun. | Jul. | Aug. | Sep. | Oct. | Nov. | Dec. |

Victims:

Events:

Name:

19___

| | Jan. | Feb. | Mar. | Apr. | May | Jun. | Jul. | Aug. | Sep. | Oct. | Nov. | Dec. |

Victims:

Events:

Name:

19___

| | Jan. | Feb. | Mar. | Apr. | May | Jun. | Jul. | Aug. | Sep. | Oct. | Nov. | Dec. |

Victims:

Events:

THINKING ERRORS: BRIDGES TO MY OFFENSE CYCLE

Thinking errors are one of the main differences between teenagers who commit sexual offenses and those who do not. You use thinking errors to connect your *pre-offense pattern* (what is happening in your life) and your *offense cycle* (what you do about it) just like the bridge connects the two banks of a stream.

Frankie, for example, is having trouble in school. He doesn't really have any close buddies, so he spends a lot of time alone. He doesn't like how he looks. His pre-offense pattern worksheet looks like this:

> **Life Events:** Having trouble in school
>
> **Behaviors:** Spending lots of time alone
>
> **Feelings:** Ugly, rejected, lonely

Julio (who goes to a different school) is also having trouble, spends a lot of time by himself, and feels lonely, ugly, and rejected. Frankie is a sex offender; Julio is not. One of the differences is in how they think about their situations.

Julio thinks:

Maybe if I ask the teacher for help, I'll understand and my grades will get better.

I gotta meet some more kids so I can find some friends who will like me.

I ain't givin' up.

So what if I'm ugly—it's what's on the inside that counts.

Maybe I can get a job so I can buy some real sharp clothes so I won't look like a nerd.

I can make people laugh, so they'll want to be around me.

Frankie thinks:

The teachers all hate me, school sucks, they just want to get me kicked out.

I'll never be good at school.

I'm just not nerdy enough for them—I don't have a computer brain.

Clubs and sports are just for popular kids, not me.

People just make fun of me anyway.

I'll never have any girlfriends or good buddies.

Life is boring, there is nothing to do.

I screw up everything—there's just no point in trying.

Nobody cares, why should I?

Then Frankie went a little further. He began thinking that he always felt better when he masturbated, but he was still lonely. Then he thought about who he could be with so he wouldn't be lonely: "Alan likes me, but he's only four. I always feel really good when I play with him. I tell him what to do, and he does it. Maybe I can babysit for him and we can play special games." The connection between Frankie's *pre-offense pattern* and his *offense cycle* are his thinking errors:

Frankie's thinking errors:

It won't hurt anybody.

I won't get caught, and if I do, I'll deny it and nobody will believe such a little kid.

It feels so good, how can it be wrong?

Just this once.

He won't tell, I'll be gentle.

It felt good when it happened to me.

If Frankie's sexual offense was rape, he might have thought something like this:

I'll really be a man when I force that girl.

Those kids at school don't know anything about sex compared to me.

She really wants it.

I don't care what she wants.

Assignment #7-E: My Thinking Errors. Now it's your turn. In the space below, list all of your thinking errors you used to connect your pre-offense pattern and your offense cycle.

_____

_____

_____

_____

_____

_____

_____

_____

_____

_____

_____

_____

_____

_____

_____

If you need more space, use a separate piece of paper.

UNDERSTANDING MY OFFENSE CYCLE

In Assignments 7-A, 7-B, and 7-C you described the major events, behaviors, thoughts, and feelings you had before your offenses started. Now it is time to understand how they make up your offense cycle. By understanding how your cycle works, you can learn to recognize when a cycle is starting and stop it before it leads to another offense.

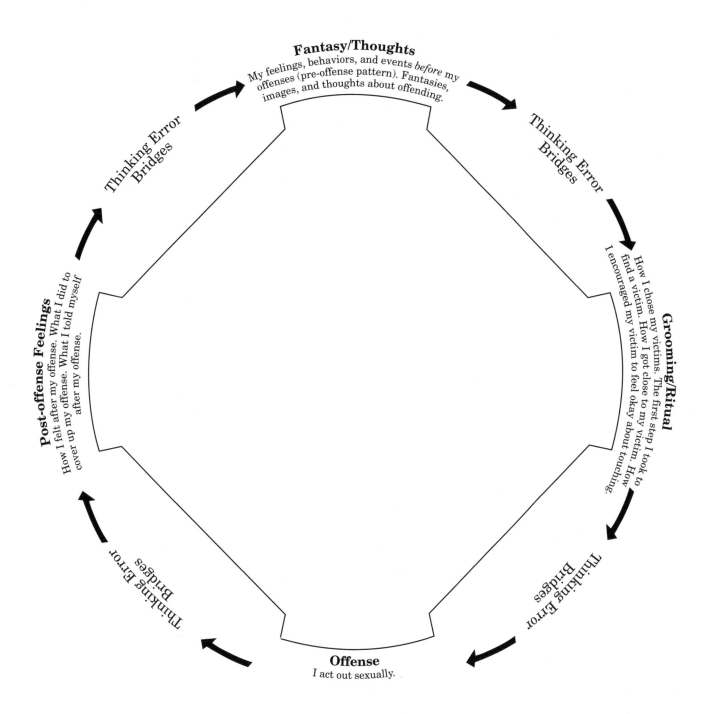

Fantasy/Thoughts
My feelings, behaviors, and events *before* my offenses (pre-offense pattern). Fantasies, images, and thoughts about offending.

Thinking Error Bridges

Thinking Error Bridges

Grooming/Ritual
How I chose my victims. The first step I took to find a victim. How I got close to my victim. How I encouraged my victim to feel okay about touching.

Thinking Error Bridges

Offense
I act out sexually.

Thinking Error Bridges

Post-offense Feelings
How I felt after my offense. What I did to cover up my offense. What I told myself after my offense.

Thinking Error Bridges

As you can see in the diagram, your offense cycle has four parts: (1) *fantasy/thoughts,* (2) *grooming or ritual process*, (3) *the actual offense*, and (4) *post-offense feelings*. The way you get from one part to another is by using thinking errors as bridges. Let's look at each of the four parts of your offense cycle and some of the thinking errors that may act as bridges for you.

1. *Fantasy/thoughts.* You are in this part of your cycle when you are thinking about offending against your victim. You are fantasizing about it, planning or daydreaming about how you want it to happen and how good it will feel. In this part of your cycle, you are setting up two of the Four Preconditions for Sexual Abuse (Chapter Five) by *motivating yourself* to offend and overcoming your *internal barriers*.

Assignment #7-F: My Fantasy/Thoughts Phase. List all of your thinking error bridges that helped you go from thinking about offending to the next part of your cycle, grooming your victim.

Possible thinking error bridges:	**List your own thinking error bridges**
Talking to him / her won't get me into trouble.	**(try not to use the ones already listed).**
It will feel so good, I'll talk her into it.	_____
I'll pretend it is an accident, he won't know.	_____
A little touching can't hurt.	_____
I'll just touch her a little.	_____
If I can get him to agree to it, I won't	_____
get in trouble.	_____

2. *Grooming or Ritual Process.* Your grooming or ritual process begins when you actually do something to make your thoughts and fantasies happen. When you are in this part of your cycle, you are setting up your victim, finding ways to get access to him or her (overcoming *external barriers* to offending), and overcoming the *victim's resistance*. At this point, you have set up all of the Four Preconditions for Sexual Abuse. Consider how Michelle, a high school sophomore with a history of molesting children, progresses from one part of her cycle to the next:

> While she is masturbating alone in her room, Michelle begins thinking about Suzie, the 8-year-old neighbor she babysits. She thinks she can get Suzie to touch her breasts and her vulva, her private parts. That night Michelle calls Suzie's mom to let her know she's available to babysit this Friday. As soon as Michelle picks up the phone, she has entered the grooming or ritual process. She has done something that may make her thoughts and fantasies a reality.

Assignment #7-G: My Grooming or Ritual Process. List all of your thinking error bridges that helped you go from grooming your victim to actually committing an offense.

Possible thinking error bridges:	**Your thinking error bridges:**
Other people have sex, why shouldn't I?	_____
She seems interested, she must want sex.	_____
He won't tell anyone, he likes me.	_____
I won't hurt her.	_____

Going a little bit further will feel good.　　_____

I'll stop if he doesn't like it.　　_____

3. ***Actual Offense.*** You enter this phase of the cycle when you commit your sexual offense: when you're touching, flashing, peeping, or threatening.

Assignment #7-H: My Actual Offenses. List all of your thinking error bridges that occurred after you committed your offenses.

Possible thinking error bridges:	**Your thinking error bridges:**
It didn't really hurt her.	_____
I'll stop, it won't happen again.	_____
He will forget about it.	_____
She asked for it, she could have said no.	_____
I didn't physically hurt him.	_____
If she wouldn't have struggled, it wouldn't have hurt.	_____
He started it by asking me to help him in the bathroom.	_____

4. ***Post-offense Feelings (Satisfaction or Remorse).*** You may have experienced a variety of feelings after you committed your offenses. The feelings could have been positive and happy, negative and unhappy, or some of both. Both feelings of satisfaction and feelings of remorse can keep your cycle going. If you experienced only sexual satisfaction, you would go right back to offending, since you liked it. Feeling guilty and upset, on the other hand, could simply make your pre-offense cycle feelings worse, therefore making it easy for you to go back to offending. It's like having a hangover that makes you feel rotten, but you drink more alcohol to try to feel better for a little while.

Assignment #7-I: My Post-offense Feelings. Describe all of the feelings you had after you committed your offenses: List all of your thinking error bridges that occurred during this part of your cycle.

Possible thinking error bridges:	**Your thinking error bridges:**
That felt good, I can't wait until I babysit again.	_____
I won't do it again.	_____
I'm an evil person.	_____
I'm going to get in trouble anyway.	_____
I'll never get caught.	_____

　　In the next chapter, you will learn about coping with your urge to offend sexually. You may feel that you must be cured by now. But there is no "cure" for sexual offending, only control. You have to learn to be aware of where you are in your cycle so urges don't take you by surprise. In Chapter Nine, you will write an Offense Prevention Plan to keep you from reoffending.

SEEMINGLY UNIMPORTANT DECISIONS (SUDS) AND HIGH RISK FACTORS (HRFS, Pronounced "Hurfs")

By now you have learned that sex offending is a complex problem, and there is no simple cause of your offending behavior. Sex offending really involves a choice, and many factors go into making choices to offend. Nobody wakes up in the morning and says, "Wow, what a good day to become a sex offender." In most cases, you sexually offend after you make a series of choices and decisions that appear by themselves to be harmless. In previous assignments in this chapter, you identified all of the thinking errors that allowed you to go from one point to the next in your offending cycle. Later on you will also learn about your "maintenance cycles" that include behaviors that are similar to sexual offending, although the choice of negative actions is different.

This section helps you learn new tools for identifying the small, *Seemingly Unimportant Decisions (SUDs)* that can lead to sex offending. You will also learn about *High Risk Factors (HRFs)* that give you chances to offend.

SUDs: Before you committed your offense, you made several choices that helped you commit a sex offense. These choices may have looked harmless by themselves, but they were the first steps toward becoming a sex offender. SUDs often lead you toward High Risk Factors, which then lead to sex offending.

Example:

William is 16 years old and had been in treatment for two years for molesting his sister Danielle, who is now 13 years old. He had also molested several other relatives and neighbors. After he completed his treatment program, his parents continued to support him in not being around his sister without adult supervision.

One weekend about a year after completing treatment, William and his two brothers (one younger, one older) planned a camping trip at Mirror Lake. It was decided that William's sister could go because William's older brother Jason and Jason's girlfriend would supervise William. Jason assigned everyone to specific sleeping places in the tent, putting William between himself and the tent wall. The group spent the day swimming, fishing, and sunbathing, mostly having a great time. But William started to feel a little weird and depressed, like his family would never trust him. When they were all in the water, Jason kept making sure that he was between William and Danielle; the same thing when they were sunbathing on the dock. William felt lonely inside himself and a little resentful when he realized this chaperoning would never end.

After supper over the campfire, everyone was tired and decided to go to sleep, except William, who stayed up watching the fire and dozed off where he was sitting. When he woke up, he decided he'd be more comfortable in his sleeping bag. But when he went to the tent, he saw by flashlight that Jason had rolled over next to the tent wall, Jason's girlfriend was next to him, and the only open spot was next to Danielle. He spread out his sleeping bag in the open spot and crawled in. But he wasn't sleepy any more. Lying awake next to Danielle, he let his thoughts wander, remembering the times when he had sex with her. After what seemed like a long time, he reached over and just lightly touched her breasts through her t-shirt, then let his hand slip down lower under her clothes when she didn't stir. Danielle woke up and sleepily went out to the latrine. William turned over and let himself fall asleep before she came back.

In looking at this example, here are some of the SUDs that William identified as leading him towards his reoffense (relapse):

SUDs:

1. Staying up late after everyone else went to bed.
2. Deciding *not* to wake up his brother.
3. Putting his sleeping bag down next to his sister.

HRFs: HRFs are any places, feelings, thoughts, or events that make it more likely that you will commit a sex offense or other hurtful behavior. To decide whether something is a HRF, ask yourself, "If everything went wrong right now, would I be more likely to reoffend?" HRFs can include your feelings, thoughts, and beliefs. They can also be things outside you, such as places where kids are (playgrounds, video arcades, malls), babysitting situations, and things that are outside of your direct control. Spending a night at a friend's house may be a HRF if the friend has a younger brother or sister (or even a same-age brother or sister if your offenses include acting out against others your own age). Going to a party may be a HRF if you have a drinking problem and are more likely to drink alcohol or use drugs at the party. If you have exposed yourself to someone in the woods, going for a walk alone in the woods could be a HRF. Feeling lonely, angry, or bored can be a HRF, because these feelings often influence your SUDs and lead to offending behaviors.

Here are some of the HRFs that William identified:

HRFs:

1. Going on an overnight campout with his sister.
2. Feeling lonely and resentful about being chaperoned.
3. Sleeping in the same tent as his sister.
4. Lying awake thinking about past sexual experiences with his sister.

As you can see, SUDs and HRFs often overlap, and SUDs can easily lead to HRFs, and sometimes HRFs (such as William feeling lonely and resentful) can lead to SUDs (such as staying up late after everyone else went to bed). The idea is to come up with as many SUDs and HRFs as you can, so you can avoid making decisions that lead you closer to offending. If you have gone this far in *Pathways*, you probably are trying pretty hard to avoid reoffending.

Assignment #7-J: Pick one of your offenses, and come up with a list of your SUDs and HRFs. Review your lists with your counselor or treatment group.

SUDs:

1.
2.
3.
4.
5.

HRFs:

1.
2.
3.
4.
5.

PREVENTING YOUR NEXT SEX OFFENSE

As you can tell, some of the SUDs and HRFs look like no big deal when taken by themselves. SUDs are tricky, because they look *unimportant*. Your job is to pay close attention and learn how they might lead to offending. One way to do this is to think about how your next offense might happen. This involves you using a negative imagination to think about how you might possibly commit another offense. You may not like doing this, but thinking about how a new offense *could* happen in order to prevent it will not *make* it happen. You have the power to intervene in your feelings and change your SUDs to prevent yourself from reoffending. By thinking about how you could commit another offense, you will be better able to identify your SUDs and HRFs.

Assignment #7-K: In the space below, describe how your next offense might happen. Use your imagination and describe the SUDs and HRFs that could lead to another offense. Describe what might be happening in your life and how those events affect your mood and feelings.

_____

_____

_____

_____

_____

_____

_____

_____

_____

_____

_____

_____

_____

_____

_____

_____

_____

_____

_____

_____

_____

_____

If you need more space, use a separate piece of paper.

MAINTENANCE CYCLES

One of the most important parts of the *Pathways* workbook process is to understand how your day-to-day behavior can lead you back to offending in the future. In *Pathways*, you have been encouraged to learn new responsible behaviors, even when they may not seem directly related to your sexual behavior. Keep in mind, your sexual behavior is controlled by your brain. In order to change your sexual behavior, you have to change the way you think about situations, and you have to *learn and demonstrate* responsible, caring behavior in all areas of your life. In this part of *Pathways*, you will learn how other problem behaviors (such as fighting, stealing, breaking rules, and hurting animals) are very similar to sex offending.

Maintenance cycles are patterns of behavior that keep you reacting to life events in hurtful and self-centered ways. They usually occur *within* your offense cycle and help keep your offense cycle going. The only real difference between maintenance cycles and the offending cycle you just learned about is that maintenance cycles involve *other* negative actions, not sex offending. Your brain, however, is reacting to situations in just the same way as when you are offending. In order to stop being a sex offender, you have to learn how to stop your maintenance cycles. Look at the example of a maintenance cycle chart on the next page. Think about what the steps of *your* maintenance cycle would look like.

Consider what Allen, a 12-year-old offender, learned about his patterns of behavior:

> I was in science class in my second period of the day when a kid behind me called me a pervert. I felt bad and angry, but what could I do about it? I felt my first tinge of victimizing behavior a few minutes after he called me the name. I started feeling fed up right afterwards. I then started planning my action of how I would get back at him for calling me a pervert. I came to group later that same day. Then I got angry at someone in group and took out my previous anger by calling *him* a pervert. I felt good for about five minutes after I called him the name, then I felt guilty about what I did and promised myself I wouldn't do it again. But I worked it out with the group on how it all started and instead of pushing my feelings away, I got to talk about how it felt to be called a bad name.

Assignment #7-L: In the space below, describe one situation you have been in during the past three months when you did something that could fit into the description of a maintenance cycle. Describe what triggered your feelings (#2. Problem Occurs), how you felt (#3. Bad Feelings), your behavior (#4. Victim Stance), your decision to take action (#5. Feeling Fed Up), and what negative action you ended up taking (#8. Negative Action). Try to cover as many of the ten points in the cycle as possible.

_____

_____

_____

_____

_____

_____

_____

_____

_____

MAINTENANCE CYCLES
DAY-TO-DAY LIFE CYCLES OF OFFENDERS

(Example)*

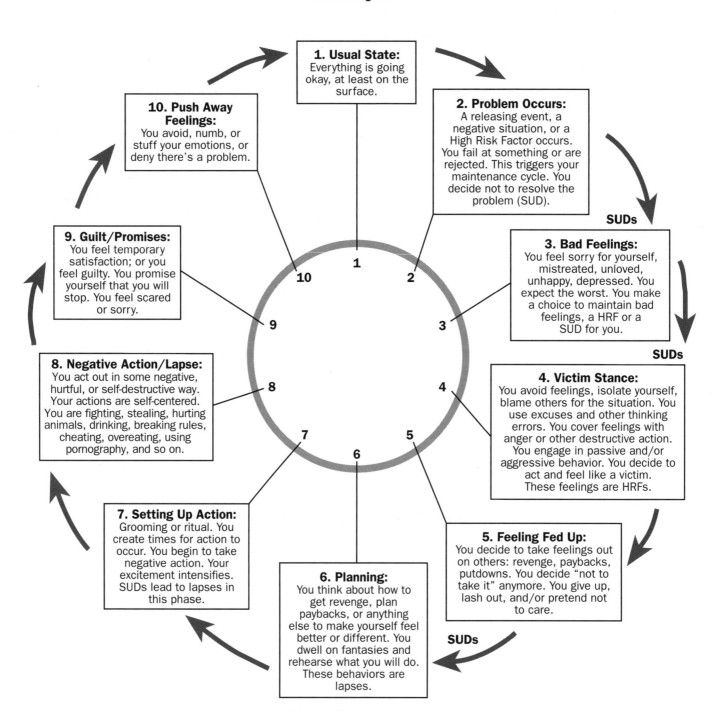

1. Usual State: Everything is going okay, at least on the surface.

2. Problem Occurs: A releasing event, a negative situation, or a High Risk Factor occurs. You fail at something or are rejected. This triggers your maintenance cycle. You decide not to resolve the problem (SUD).

SUDs

3. Bad Feelings: You feel sorry for yourself, mistreated, unloved, unhappy, depressed. You expect the worst. You make a choice to maintain bad feelings, a HRF or a SUD for you.

SUDs

4. Victim Stance: You avoid feelings, isolate yourself, blame others for the situation. You use excuses and other thinking errors. You cover feelings with anger or other destructive action. You engage in passive and/or aggressive behavior. You decide to act and feel like a victim. These feelings are HRFs.

5. Feeling Fed Up: You decide to take feelings out on others: revenge, paybacks, putdowns. You decide "not to take it" anymore. You give up, lash out, and/or pretend not to care.

SUDs

6. Planning: You think about how to get revenge, plan paybacks, or anything else to make yourself feel better or different. You dwell on fantasies and rehearse what you will do. These behaviors are lapses.

7. Setting Up Action: Grooming or ritual. You create times for action to occur. You begin to take negative action. Your excitement intensifies. SUDs lead to lapses in this phase.

8. Negative Action/Lapse: You act out in some negative, hurtful, or self-destructive way. Your actions are self-centered. You are fighting, stealing, hurting animals, drinking, breaking rules, cheating, overeating, using pornography, and so on.

9. Guilt/Promises: You feel temporary satisfaction; or you feel guilty. You promise yourself that you will stop. You feel scared or sorry.

10. Push Away Feelings: You avoid, numb, or stuff your emotions, or deny there's a problem.

These steps may not be exactly the same or in this exact order for every offender.

Assignment #7-M: With your counselor or treatment group, discuss your cycle in the assignment above and come up with at least three ways of interrupting your cycle *in a healthy way* during its early stages. List your ideas below.

1. _____

_____

_____

2. _____

_____

_____

3. _____

_____

_____

NOTE: The key to interrupting your maintenance cycles is to develop the support and skills needed to deal with your feelings and problems in a direct and healthy way. To do this, you have to learn to express your feelings *in non-hurting ways* . Working on developing a support system will help you accomplish this goal.

In Chapter Eight, you will learn about coping with your urges to offend sexually. You may feel that you must be cured by now. But remember, there is no "cure" for sexual offending, only control. You have to learn to be aware of where you are in your cycles so urges don't take you by surprise. In Chapter Nine, you will write an Offense Prevention Plan to help you interrupt your cycles before they lead you back to sexual offending.

NOTES ON MY MAINTENANCE AND OFFENSE CYCLES

CHAPTER EIGHT

CONTROLLING MY URGE TO OFFEND

This chapter is about your sexual feelings; it might be the most difficult one to complete, because you may feel ashamed, or embarrassed, or fear that people will make fun of you. You may never have had the opportunity to talk openly with others about your sexual feelings, masturbation patterns, or sexual activity with partners. You might have joked with your friends about your sexual "conquests," but almost never really talked about your failures, concerns, or problems. As a teenage sex offender, you may have tried to find nonsexual explanations for your sexual behavior because it is easier to say, "I raped the little girl to get revenge on her parents," than it is to say, "I raped the little girl because she turned me on sexually." Revenge sounds like normal "macho" behavior, while you might feel that being sexually turned on by a seven-year-old is "perverted."

Many teenage sex offenders' "urge" to offend comes from being sexually aroused. A large number of teenage offenders admit during the treatment process that they have ongoing urges to offend that they don't know how to control. This chapter describes some methods that are used to control these kinds of urges.

Consider the experience of Anna, a 13-year-old girl who has been learning about her sexual feelings and urges:

> When I started puberty it got a lot harder to control my sexual urges, especially since I had been abused and had abused children when I was younger. I found myself thinking about my earlier experiences with other children a lot more, then it was harder because when I went through puberty my sexual hormones got stronger. My sexual urges got very strong, and it was hard to control them. It was very hard even though I did survive through it. I could understand how someone could try to ignore their sexual feelings and not succeed. Please, for your sake, learn the skills in this chapter to help you through puberty without offending. I have been in treatment for a year now, and I am much better at controlling my urges than I used to be.

Your sexual urges may come from either *healthy* or *deviant* sexual fantasies or daydreams about sexual contact. Sexual fantasies happen when you let your thoughts wander toward sexual images. You may not at first be aware that you are thinking these sexual thoughts, or even that you are thinking at all. *Healthy* sexual fantasies are sexual thoughts and images that involve *loving, caring*, and *respectful contact with a willing partner who is close in age to you*. You feel sexual toward the person in a healthy fantasy because of how much you *care* about him or her. Healthy relationships involve feelings of concern, friendship, and affection for your partner, including talking about *and using* birth control as an expression of responsible behavior.

In *unhealthy* fantasies and relationships, you care about the people only because they let you have sex with them or because you hope they will. In reality, you care mostly about the sex, not about the person. *Deviant* sexual fantasies are sexual thoughts and images that include using tricks, bribes, or prostitution (paying or getting money or presents in exchange for sex). They involve partners who are more than 3 years older or younger than you, or who don't understand much about sex. The sexual activities may include dominating or controlling the other person (making the other person do what you want without caring about his or her feelings). It may involve sex that causes physical pain to you or the other person. Deviant sexual fantasies and behaviors may involve using weapons or other threatening objects, tying up the other person or your being tied up, and other sexual acts with someone you don't care about.

One general way to help prevent yourself from offending again is to change your sexual urges by changing your fantasies. Work on replacing deviant sexual fantasies with healthy ones. Every time you let yourself wander into a deviant sexual fantasy, you come closer to reoffending. When you masturbate to your deviant sexual fantasy, the pleasure you get encourages you to do it more, and moves you even closer to reoffending. Every time you use a healthy sexual fantasy, you take yourself further away from reoffending. Your counselor can teach you ways of practicing healthy fantasies and stopping deviant fantasies. Below are some examples of treatment methods that are used.

Two kinds of techniques you can use to control your urge to offend are *impulse control* and *arousal control*. *Impulse control* concentrates on distracting your thoughts when you're feeling the impulse to commit an offense. *Arousal control* concentrates on changing your sexual feelings. If you have any questions about these techniques and where to get the training to use them, ask your group leader for help.

IMPULSE CONTROL

Impulse control is an emergency stopgap measure, like a Bandaid. These techniques will not totally change or eliminate your urges, but they will help you control some urges when they occur.

Thought-stopping. In this method, you yell "STOP!" inside your head every time an offending fantasy or urge occurs. It also helps to wear a rubber band around your wrist so that you can snap it hard when an urge occurs. The idea is to interrupt the urge before you act on it, or derail the train of thought before it becomes a runaway locomotive. This technique works better when you replace the offending thoughts with their opposite. For instance when you think, "She wants me to have sex with her," you'd yell "STOP!" Then snap your rubber band. Then you might think, "Sex is the furthest thing from her mind right now—I need to respect that."

Impulse Charting. In this method, you carry a small notebook or journal with you at all times and make a note in it whenever you have an urge. Stopping to write in the journal will interrupt the urge and give you time to get it under control.

Thought-switching. This is a way of making your mind think of something else, instead of dwelling on the sexual urge. For example, you might think of what it would be like in detention whenever you have the urge to offend. This takes away the power of the urge, and helps you devote your attention elsewhere.

AROUSAL CONTROL

Arousal control techniques are harder to learn and require much more practice. If you use them over a long period of time, they can help reduce your urge to offend. **You must be trained and monitored by an experienced sex-offender treatment specialist before using these techniques.** *Do not attempt to use these techniques without training.*

Masturbatory Reconditioning. This technique involves developing (with your counselor's help) age-appropriate, nonviolent, consenting fantasies you can masturbate to when you're alone. You either keep a journal of your masturbation sessions, or tape record them (speaking your fantasy out loud), so your counselor can make sure you're doing it the right way. This may sound very embarrassing, but you get used to it. *Masturbatory reconditioning increases your arousal to **appropriate** sexual behavior.*

Covert Sensitization(CS). In Covert Sensitization (CS), you cancel out your offending fantasies by pairing them with a thought, image, or smell that is scary, unpleasant, or disgusting. You make tapes of your offending urges, then add a scene that upsets you, like being arrested. Then you think of a scene that rewards you with something pleasant for not offending. This technique can work well when you also use Masturbatory Reconditioning to help you find appropriate images to replace your offending fantasies.

A CS tape typically starts with a relaxation exercise, then moves on to a fantasy scenario that stops just at the point of offending and substitutes an upsetting ending. Then you create a positive replacement scene where you *don't* offend and experience positive feelings. If your fantasy changes to a different offending scene, you make a new tape, again pairing your fantasy with a scene that upsets or frightens you, or with an obnoxious smell, like ammonia, and replace the offending scene with a positive one. Roger's scenario below is a good example of the fantasy, negative ending, and positive scene portions of a CS tape.

Offending Fantasy: There's this girl I met, she's a couple of years younger than me. She seems kind of simple, maybe naive, and I'm very attracted to her. She has talked to me a few times and seems to like me. Today I'm feeling very horny—how can I get to be alone with her? I decide to follow her home through the park. As she enters the park I run up and grab her from behind. She tries to scream, but I clamp my hand over her mouth and push her to the ground, while unzipping my pants. STOP!

Scary scene: I immediately come to my senses and glance around me. Just off to my right I see a policeman drawing his revolver and running toward me. I let the girl go and try to zip my pants but can't find the zipper. My penis has shriveled up to nothing. She starts screaming hysterically as a crowd of people quickly gathers around me. People are yelling "Rapist! Rapist! Pervert!" while others are screaming at me. The policeman grabs me coldly and wrenches my arms behind my back. I feel the cold metal of handcuffs on my wrists. I am so ashamed and embarrassed! I lift my head slightly and notice that several of my friends are in the crowd staring at me. Worst of all, my parents are working their way toward me from the back of the crowd. My friends are shaking their heads and I hear one of them saying he didn't know I was a "pervert." I feel disgusted with myself and totally alone.

Positive scene: I see the girl go into the park. I turn around and head back toward school. There's a pickup basketball game in the parking lot and I ask if I can play. The guys rotate me in and I score two baskets. I feel pretty good, and one of the guys says I can play on his team any time.

Boredom Tapes. With boredom tapes your counselor gives you a very boring assignment of reading or making up very boring stories about your offending. Then you make tapes using a cassette tape recorder so your counselor can check them. With Boredom Tapes (also called Verbal Satiation), the idea is that you will get so bored with your offending fantasy that you will no longer get aroused by it. Often, your counselor will ask you to make several hours of tapes every week. While this might sound boring and dull, it is a lot better than spending time in prison or having sexual behavior problems when you are older. All you really need for this is some privacy, a tape recorder, and some blank tapes.

Vicarious Sensitization (VS). This is a new treatment method that involves listening to a tape that describes your sexual offending behavior or fantasy. Then after a few minutes, you switch to watching a scary video showing what might happen to you if you continue offending. The tapes switch back and forth from your offense to the possible consequences so that you will associate your offending with something scary and negative. This technique requires expensive equipment, and your counselor may not be able to offer it to you.

All of these techniques take work on your part. You are really learning how to control your body and your fantasies. *It takes practice.* Boys may be asked or required to go through a "phallometric assessment" using an instrument called a "penile plethysmograph" before and after you use these techniques. During a penile plethysmograph evaluation you sit in a private room listening to tapes or maybe looking at slides. Your arousal is shown by the increase in your penis size (tumescence) during the tapes or slides, and it is measured by a machine connected to a gauge that looks like a rubber or metal band. It might sound uncomfortable, but many teenagers have gone through it and have found it to be a good way to measure the progress they have made at controlling their arousal. Plethysmography is not used with girls because it is simply harder to measure female sexual arousal. However, you girls can still report on your sexual arousal, and you, like the many other teenage girls who already have, can use all of the arousal control techniques listed in this chapter to help you control your sexual feelings.

Kylen, a 16-year-old sex offender, succeeded at making a huge change in his arousal pattern, but it took a lot of work to make the changes, as he writes.

> When I first went through a plethysmograph assessment I got aroused to almost everything. When I was asked to control my arousal, I couldn't do it at all. During the two months before Christmas I spent almost all of my free time doing CS tapes. I got so bored and tired I would fall asleep doing the tapes. All in all, I did 120 hours of CS. I used to go into my group and put the completed tapes in a big pile on the floor, and they would pick them out to listen to. About a month after I finished the 120 hours, I went through another plethysmograph evaluation. I was not sure how I would do, but I found out that I can now keep my arousal to offending situations down to almost nothing. I was very happy that I actually made it work for me.

Remember, these techniques have been used successfully by many teenagers and adults to control their sexual behavior. Again, they must be taught to you by a trained counselor, and they may have some emotional side-effects which should be explained to you.

On the next page is a sheet called a "Fantasy Tracking Form." Using this form is up to you and your counselor, but it is very helpful when you use any of the sexual arousal control techniques. You can use this tracking form to help you feel more at ease discussing your sexual fantasies (thoughts) and your masturbation habits and to provide information for your counseling. Don't worry about what others will think — nearly all teenagers, both boys and girls, masturbate. You should fill out the form every time you masturbate, as well as every time you have an inappropriate sexual thought. Your counselor or group leader may have copied and handed out this form separately, so you may not need to fill out this one. Remember to be honest; dishonesty wastes your treatment time and energy and only leads to ineffective treatment, reoffenses, and more pain and trouble for you, your family, and the people you abuse.

Name:_____

Fantasy Tracking

Date	Day/Time	Other Person's Name & Age	Type of Behavior	Masturbation Yes/No

If you need more space, use a separate piece of paper.

Directions: Use this form to keep track of your sexual fantasies and / or masturbation patterns.

Check with your counselor for other instructions before using this form.

CHAPTER NINE

CREATING MY OFFENSE PREVENTION PLAN

Now that you understand your pre-offense pattern and offense cycle, you are ready to work on your Offense Prevention Plan—**IF** you have done a good job on Chapter Seven. If you're not sure about anything in Chapter Seven, ask your group leader for help in doing those assignments again. You have to understand and be able to recognize the thoughts, feelings, behaviors, and events that lead up to your offending behaviors before you can take steps to get out of your offending cycle.

MAKING A PREVENTION PLAN

Look at Daniel Brown's Offense Prevention Plan on pages 82 and 83. On the first page, there are two columns labeled *Warning Sign* and *Prevention Plan*. In the left hand column, under *Warning Sign*, he has listed his feelings, thoughts, behaviors, and events that lowered his barriers to offending and led up to his offenses.

Assignment #9-A: My Warning Signs. Turn to the blank Offense Prevention Plan page, fill in your name and the date at the top, and list your warning signs. Consider all possible warning signs: motivations (urges), internal barriers (feelings), external barriers (lifestyle), and victim's resistance (relationships with victims). If you need help, go back to Chapter Seven and review your *pre-offense pattern* and the *preoccupation* section of your offense cycle. Also review your maintenance cycle (from Assignment #7-L) and the sample maintenance cycle chart. Any time you recognize any of these feelings, thoughts, events, and behaviors happening in your life, you then start your Prevention Plan.

Now look at the right hand column on Daniel's Prevention Plan. He has listed the practical things he'll do to prevent himself from going deeper into his offense cycle.

Assignment #9-B: My Prevention Plan. Turn to the Prevention Plan page where you listed your warning signs. Across from each of your warning signs, write what your new response will be, what you will *do* to prevent yourself from going deeper into your cycle whenever you recognize that warning sign. Make it as practical and concrete as you can. Talking to someone who can help you (a counselor, therapist, teacher, parole or probation officer) should be one of your responses. If you are learning techniques to control your urges to offend, they should be in your Prevention Plan too. You may need to do this assignment more than once and discuss it with your group and your counselor.

On the second page of his Prevention Plan, Daniel has listed his *high-risk situations*, the things he does when he's beginning his offense cycle: choosing his victim, getting close to him or her, denying his feelings. Your *high-risk situations* include the ways you get over your internal and external barriers to offending, and your grooming or ritual process.

Assignment #9-C: My High-risk Situations. List *your* high-risk situations on the second page of your Prevention Plan.

At the bottom of the second page of Daniel's Prevention Plan, his parents, his uncle who lives with them, his school counselor, and his parole officer have all signed. By signing, they promised that they would help Daniel make the plan work, for example, by not asking him to babysit and by helping him find a summer job that wasn't around younger kids.

After you have talked over your Prevention Plan with your group leader and the members of the group, ask your parents, foster parents, other relatives, counselor, group home staff, probation or parole officer, and/or any other important people in your life to read and sign it. Make sure they know what everything in it means so they can really help you with it.

The final step of the Offense Prevention Plan is up to you—you have to **use it!**

Assignment #9-D: Using the Plan. *Read your Offense Prevention Plan **every** day!* Ask yourself: "Did I feel or do any of these things today?" When the answer is yes, start your Prevention Plan to get out of your offense cycle.

Some of your warning signs and all of your high-risk situations may be considered *lapses* in preventing offenses. A *lapse* is what happens when you slip a little bit. Lapses can pile up until you *relapse* (reoffend). For Daniel, a lapse might be having a sexual fantasy about the younger kids next door. He hasn't yet reoffended, but having the fantasy is a step on the way toward reoffending. He might think, "It's no use— I'll always have these thoughts. I might as well just give up and go ahead with touching kids sexually." That's a thinking error. You may have a lapse, especially if you ignore one of your warning signs, but don't give up. You can control your urges, but it takes time and practice. ***Don't give up!***

OFFENSE PREVENTION PLAN

NAME: Daniel Brown   DATE: 2/23/96

WARNING SIGN	PREVENTION PLAN
1. Feeling depressed, unwanted or treated unfairly.	1. Talk to someone about my feelings. Stay active, don't let things get me down!
2. Feeling aroused by young children.	2. Stay away from children. Find people my age or older to do things with. Use covert sensitization.
3. Increase in sexual feelings and urges.	3. Use negative thoughts and images to stop fantasies of offending. Think about what would happen if I got caught again. Write down how it would feel to be the victim. Masturbate only to mutual fantasies involving partners my own age.
4. Increase in stress. Having other problems in my life like getting kicked out of school, abused, etc.	4. Use relaxation techniques. Take care of myself, take time out for positive activities. Talk to others about my feelings!
5. Having an "I don't care" attitude.	5. Accept feedback from others. Make something positive happen, don't let self fall into offense cycle.
6. Feeling bored.	6. Call a friend. Ask parents to do something fun. Do homework or help out around the house. Go outside and exercise. Don't let myself be lazy! Stay active with others my age. Go to dances, sports events, school activities, or church. Call a friend my own age!

HIGH-RISK SITUATIONS TO AVOID AT ALL COSTS

1. Being alone with my niece

2. Being alone with any young children

3. Using any drugs or alcohol

4. Babysitting

5. Working at a job where I am responsible for children or have access to children

I have read the entire offense prevention plan described on these two pages and have had an opportunity to ask questions. I have also had an opportunity to provide further input and suggestions to improve the plan. I agree to support this plan fully, and I will do everything possible to make the plan work. (This plan should be signed by as many people as possible who are involved in your life, including your parents, extended family, probation and parole officers, foster parents, and group home staff.)

James S. Brown   _2/23/96_
(Signature)   (Date)

Consuelo V. Brown   _2/23/96_
(Signature)   (Date)

Victor M. Nugas (uncle)   _2/23/96_
(Signature)   (Date)

Alice F. Johnsen (school counselor)   _2/28/96_
(Signature)   (Date)

Frank K. DeAngelo (parole officer)   _2/28/96_
(Signature)   (Date)

MY OFFENSE PREVENTION PLAN

NAME: _____   DATE: _____

WARNING SIGN	PREVENTION PLAN
1.	1.
2.	2.
3.	3.
4.	4.
5.	5.
6.	6.
7.	7.
8.	8.
9.	9.
10.	10.

HIGH-RISK SITUATIONS TO AVOID AT ALL COSTS

1.

2.

3.

4.

5.

I have read the entire offense prevention plan described on these two pages and have had an opportunity to ask questions. I have also had an opportunity to provide further input and suggestions to improve the plan. I agree to support this plan fully, and I will do everything possible to make the plan work. (This plan should be signed by as many people as possible who are involved in your life, including your parents, extended family, probation and parole officers, foster parents, and group home staff.)

_____   _____
(Signature)   (Date)

_____   _____
(Signature)   (Date)

_____   _____
(Signature)   (Date)

_____   _____
(Signature)   (Date)

_____   _____
(Signature)   (Date)

CHAPTER TEN

WHAT IF I WAS ABUSED?

Part of your treatment involves finding out whether you have been sexually abused. Not every sex offender has been sexually abused. Most victims of past sexual abuse never commit a sexual offense. ***Having been sexually abused is never an excuse for committing a sexual offense.***

Maybe you do not remember any experience that felt abusive. Many victims of sexual abuse totally block out all memory of it until they become adults. But even though the memory of the events is blocked, the effects of being abused still bother them, and they don't know why. Offenders sometimes remember their abuse only after they begin learning about victims. Bruce, a 39-year-old sex offender, had an experience like that while he was in treatment:

> Last week, after watching the videotape on child abuse during the group session, I found myself feeling kind of sad. When I got home later that night I found myself feeling teary. After thinking for a few minutes I found myself remembering being sexually abused by my older brother when I was six years old. I don't know why I blocked it out. If anybody had ever asked me about being sexually abused before last week, I would have honestly said I had never been abused. Now that I can remember what happened I know that I was very confused and scared at the time it happened. I also know a little bit more about why I have never really liked myself very much, and why I have often felt like committing suicide for no apparent reason. That experience was the beginning of my loss of self-esteem.

Again, not every adolescent sex offender has been sexually abused. If you have not been sexually abused, you are not alone. Sex offenders can get the idea of committing this offense from other sources, not just from experiencing abuse. If you were not abused, go back and review Chapter Four. Pay special attention to the story "Donnie's Brother Remembers" and the homework assignments before going on to Chapter Eleven.

Many different types of abuse can be just as harmful as sexual abuse. For example, physical abuse can often result in permanent scars and long-lasting fear. Verbal abuse, such as constant criticism, can also result in feeling helpless or bad about yourself. Think about how your life experiences have affected your feelings and behaviors now.

Like Bruce, you may have started to remember an experience from your childhood while learning in treatment about victims. You may feel confused or scared and unsure whether what you remember was abuse or whether it really happened. The first step in dealing with your own abuse is to get the courage to talk to others about what happened to you. Talking about it can be very hard and very scary for some of the reasons listed below:

1. **People will call me "fag," "queer," or "lezzie."** Since most known sex offenders are male, many male victims of sexual abuse are worried that they will be called names by others who might find out about it. This reaction is sometimes called "queer fear" (homophobia). Girls who were molested by female offenders have the same worry. But being sexually abused by a person of the same sex (or even of the opposite sex) does not *make* you a homosexual, even if your body responded sexually at the time. Sexual abuse does not "cause" homosexuality. People *discover* their sexual orientation by realizing who they feel closest to most of the time, or who they fall in love with. People are not only "straight" (heterosexual) or "gay" (homosexual)—they can be "bisexual," loving men sometimes and

women sometimes. Having gay feelings is not the end of the world; most gay people live successful, productive lives.

2. **Nobody will believe that I was molested.** If you've lied about your own offending, you're probably afraid that people will think you're still lying, especially if the person who abused you was female. Some people believe that girls or women could never be molesters, because we almost never read or hear about it. But researchers are discovering that some girls and women *do* molest both boys and girls. It is abuse, and there are people who will believe you.

3. **It was just sex—it wasn't abusive.** Some boys learn the attitude that having sex with a girl or woman is proof of their manhood; so the younger they do it, the more "manly" they are. You may secretly feel pride in how "mature" you are, or joke about how "lucky" you were to "score" so young. The person who abused you, or someone you may have tried to talk to about this experience may even have told you these things. Girls may also see sexual contact with older boys as "proof" of their maturity. Whether you are male or female, you could have had sexual contact with an older person or an adult and not think it was abusive. If you were molested in "gentle" or "loving" ways, or in situations that were disguised as medical exams, health care, or "normal" nurturing, you may have a hard time identifying your experiences as sexually abusive. Whether a sexual contact is abusive depends on what kind of power or persuasion was used to get you to participate and on how old you were at the time. To help you sort it out, discuss all of your sexual experiences with your counselor. He or she will help you decide if any experience was sexually abusive.

4. **I can handle it—I'm not a baby.** Men and boys in our society are often taught to "tough it out" rather than ask for help. Males are frequently told to "handle it" rather than openly share their hurt, sadness, or other feelings. Some girls and women are taught to expect abuse as part of their role in life. Sometimes girls are taught keep their feelings to themselves and just go along with what a male says. They may learn that there's no point in complaining, that no one will help or protect them, or teach them how to protect themselves. Unfortunately, hiding or avoiding these feelings only makes both boys and girls feel more isolated and lonely. The fact that you have offended against someone else shows that you can't "handle it"—and you shouldn't have to even try handling it alone. You did not deserve to be abused. No one deserves to be abused. You did deserve to get caring help from adults if you went through sexual or physical abuse.

5. **I'll be punished for being bad.** Boys are taught to be self-reliant and strong, and some boys are fearful that they will be blamed for not fighting off the abuser or avoiding the situation entirely. Girls are taught that they are responsible for any sexual activity, that it is their job to prevent it, and if they don't, that it is their fault. Girls are often blamed for being in the "wrong" place, for "leading on" the offender, or for acting "seductive." Whether you are male or female, you will not be punished for being victimized. The only person responsible for the abuse is the offender.

6. **I feel guilty for not stopping the abuse.** Some boys and girls blame themselves and feel guilty for not stopping the abuse. This guilt can lead to the victim feeling bad about themselves. Guilt is very confusing for victims of sexual abuse. Being abused is not the victim's fault: not your fault when you were a victim, and not the fault of the people you abused.

7. **I don't want to hurt my family.** Some victims of sexual abuse are afraid that if they talk about the sexual abuse their families will blame them or reject them. When the offender is a family member, the victim might be afraid of getting the offender into trouble. Sometimes victims simply decide to keep their experiences to themselves rather than "make waves" and cause trouble within their family. But the only way for both a victim and his or her family to get real help is by talking about what is really going on.

Assignment #10-A: *Being a victim.* If you believe that you went through any sexually or physically abusive or hurtful experience, please complete this assignment. In the space below describe what happened to you when you were abused.

Dates abuse happened:_____

Describe what happened:_____

_____

_____

_____

_____

_____

_____

_____

_____

_____

_____

_____

_____

_____

_____

_____

If you need more space, use a separate piece of paper.

Assignment #10-B: Describe how the abuse affected your *feelings* (some examples are numb, scared, angry, or depressed):

_____

_____

_____

_____

_____

_____

_____

_____

_____

_____

If you need more space, use a separate piece of paper.

Now let's take a look at how sexual abuse can affect your behavior. Below is a list of ways a young victim's behavior can be affected by sexual or physical abuse.

Fight:

— Breaking the law, breaking rules

— Getting into fights with others

— Fire setting

— Acting moody

— Overeating

— Throwing tantrums, "going off"

— Compulsive masturbation and sexual acting-out

— Acting extremely responsible

— Getting angry easily

— Damaging property

— Acting aggressive, taking feelings out on others

Flight:

— Running away

— Leaving home early

— Attempting suicide

— Having difficulty sleeping

— Developing some chronic physical symptoms (headache, stomachache)

— Acting withdrawn, isolating self from others

— Having nightmares

Numbing:

— Denying all feelings

— Using drugs/alcohol

— Not being able to concentrate/school problems

— Self-mutilation (hurting yourself)

— Acting depressed

— Acting rigid/avoiding discussion of abuse

— Pretending nothing is wrong

— Blocking out memories

Assignment #10-C: The Impact of Sexual Abuse on My Life: Consider the list of behaviors above. In the space below list all of the impacts you feel your abuse experiences have had on your behavior. Include all your ideas, even if they are not described in the lists above.

_____

_____

_____

_____

_____

_____

_____

_____

_____

_____

_____

_____

_____

_____

_____

_____

_____

_____

_____

_____

If you need more space, use a separate piece of paper.

Understanding and resolving your own sexual and physical abuse will take much more time and effort than can be accomplished in *Pathways*. Many victims of abuse struggle with their recovery for years—these feelings and behavior patterns won't go away overnight. For now, you've started to look at your life experiences as they relate to your offending behavior. Even though it is scary and painful to talk about it, getting it out in the open is the most important step in recovering from your experiences. Please talk with your counselor about your own abuse in greater detail so that you can develop a long-term plan for recovery.

Another reason to look at how you felt when you were a victim is so you will understand in a new way the feelings of the people you abused. In Chapter Eleven you will get a chance to apply what you've learned in this chapter about the effects of abuse to understanding how the people you abused felt and how to make amends. ***Remember that being a victim of past abuse is never an excuse for committing a sexual offense.***

CHAPTER ELEVEN

CLARIFICATION: MAKING THINGS CLEAR

Developing a clear understanding of how your victims were affected by your abusive behavior is essential to your treatment. This process is sometimes called *clarification*,[1] which means "making things clear." The clarification process helps you understand the total impact of your behavior and accept full responsibility for all your actions. Clarification is the basis for restitution to your victim. *Restitution* means doing everything you can to *restore* your victim to a state as close as possible to how he or she was before you committed your offenses. It means taking into account all the different kinds of harm your offenses caused directly to your victim and to his or her parents and anyone else involved. You cannot give restitution until you understand all the ways your actions caused harm.

Usually the clarification process starts early in treatment; it continues for a long time because it often takes lots of work to understand and accept the impact of sexual abuse on your victims. There are three steps to clarification: (1) clarification to yourself of what you've done (overcoming denial) and learning about victims; (2) clarification letters to your victim(s); and (3) meetings with your victim(s).

Clarification to Myself

You start clarification by being honest about what you did and why you did it. Then you begin learning about sexual abuse from talking with adult victims who have been in counseling and/or from remembering how you felt when you were victimized (review Chapters Four and Ten to help you). Your treatment group may watch videotapes of abuse victims talking about their experiences, or read stories of people who have been abused. In addition, your counselor and treatment group may have information and exercises like "Donnie's Brother Remembers" that can help you learn about the effects of sexual abuse.

Assignment #11-A: Preparing for Clarification. In order to get ready for the clarification process, it is time to make sure that you really are ready. Go back to page 41 in Chapter Four and on a separate piece of paper, write out the 20 questions victims may ask. Answer each question separately as if your most recent victim is asking you. Review your answers with your counselor or treatment group.

Clarification Letters to The People I Abused

You may continue the clarification process by writing a series of letters to the victims you abused and to their families. You must follow five rules in writing your clarification and later in presenting it:

1. Write the letter using language the victim can clearly understand. For example, if Mike started abusing his sister Barbara when she was four, but now she is nine, Mike would need to be careful to write his letter in language a four-to-nine year old could understand.

2. Include specific examples of your behavior, conversations, and incidents, in order to clear up any confusion and thinking errors. Explain how each act has hurt this *particular* victim. It's not enough to say "I betrayed your trust in me," because that could apply to anyone. Each clarification must be

---

[1]This chapter is based on pp. 403-422 of *Just Before Dawn* by Jan Hindman (1989, AlexAndria Associates) by permission of the author (see Readings).

unique to each victim. Your treatment group and counselor will help you make sure that you do not cause any further hurt to the person you abused when you describe your behavior, conversations, and incidents. Remember, the idea is not to make the victim re-experience the abuse, but to remember it and understand what you did without blaming themselves or feeling guilty.

3. Accept that this entire process is under the victim's control — not yours. Visiting and talking to the victims are privileges you have to earn. You earn these privileges by showing that you can do it in a way that truly helps the victim. It's not the victim's job to "forgive" you or let you off the hook. But it is your job to make things better for the victim by letting him or her know it wasn't the victim's fault, explaining why you committed the offense, showing that you understand in detail all the harm you've caused, and making restitution in ways that give the victim all the power.

4. Write a separate clarification letter to the parents of the person you abused. Normally, the letter to the parents is presented first, and if it is accepted, a meeting with the victim may be scheduled later. Sometimes, it is also a good idea to write letters of apology to other family members who have been affected by your abusive behavior. This is especially important when the victim is a family member. As always, **never send any letter without your treatment group and counselor's approval.**

5. If you have victimized more than one person, you will need to go through this process with each victim and his or her family. This might seem like a lot of work, and it is. It is one of the consequences of your actions, however, and many teenagers just like you have found that going through this clarification process is the most healing part of treatment.

When the person you abused is a family member, writing your letter is an especially necessary step. With a letter, the victim has something concrete to hold onto, to remind himself/herself that it really happened, that it wasn't his/her fault, and that you're doing your best to make restitution. Your counselor and/or your treatment group should always review your letters. **Never send a letter to your victim's parents or your victim without your counselor's and treatment group's permission!** You will probably have to rewrite your letter several times before it is ready to send. Clarification letters and possible presentations to your victims should include:

— A meaningful greeting that does not make light conversation or ask questions (questions demand an answer, and by your behavior, you've given up the right to demand anything from your victim).

— A statement that the victim is in control of reading this letter or hearing this presentation, although in the past during the secret touching, you were in control.

— A statement of responsibility ("I did it, it was my fault") and that the victim did the good, right, and brave thing in telling about the secret touching.

— A description of the person you abused, paying attention to his or her positive qualities you used to manipulate him/her into sexual contact.

— What you did, in detail (include grooming behaviors and clear up all thinking errors and lies).

— How you used the victim's good qualities to get sexual contact.

— All the ways you can think of that your behavior damaged the person you abused, in detail (include damage to relationships with family members and friends, future harm to his/her feelings and attitudes as he/she grows up, and the kinds of places he/she might be afraid of because of your abuse).

— Why you did it ("I was selfish"), why sexual contact is so valuable that you would steal it ("it feels really wonderful when it is kept special to share when you're a grown-up with a person you pick"), what it is about you that you would do it ("I break rules, I don't think about other people's feelings"), and why the person you abused is unable to *consent*, regardless of what he/she said during the abuse.

— Description of how treatment is helping you now.

— An offer to answer any questions the person you abused may ask and to help in any way possible to aid in his/her recovery from the abuse.

— Your commitment to continuing treatment and nonvictimizing behavior.

It is often **not** okay to send the letters you write to the people you abused or to their parents. They may have stated that they want no contact at all with you, and you *must* respect that boundary; if you don't respect their wishes, you show that you haven't learned enough about respect in your treatment. Or there may be a court order or a condition of your probation or parole that prohibits you from contacting the people you abused or their families. Your probation counselor or parole officer may be able to make an exception if the contact is to help the victim and to continue your treatment. This is why you must *never* send your letters to them without getting permission first from your counselor and your group. But even when you will not be sending your letters, writing them also helps you to become more sensitive to the needs and feelings of the people you abused.

Sometimes instead of a clarification letter your counselor may ask you to make video tapes in your counselor's office that serve the same purpose as a clarification letter. The video can sometimes be more realistic, and the victims often can have an easier time understanding when the words are spoken on tape, rather than in a letter. Videotaped or audiotaped clarifications can also be used in place of face-to-face meetings when the victim lives far away, or when the victim wants to hear what you have to say, but doesn't want to meet with you.

Below is the first draft of a letter Brandon, a 14-year-old sex offender, wrote to his victim, his cousin Becky, age 10:

Dear Becky,

How's it going? I know how you must feel about me and I'm sorry you have to feel that way. If there is anything I can do to repay you from all the trouble you've gone through I'll be glad to help out. I know this might sound kinda weird but I'm glad you told on me. It's made me a better person. I've been going to counseling since December and I have learned a lot. There are a lot of other kids going to counseling with me who have similar problems. We are taught to be open about our offenses. It was hard for me at first but now it's easy for me to talk about it. We are also taught to get our problems out and find a solution for them. I know we won't be able to have the same kind of relationship as we had before, but I guess that's the breaks. I also want to say I'm sorry for all of the pain you had to go through. I don't know if you knew whether or not I went to detention but I did go for 30 days. I also got two years of probation. I want you to know I wish this would've never have happened and that it won't ever happen again. Also if it wasn't for you I wouldn't ever have gotten help for my problems. I hope one day I will be able to face you in person and tell you I am sorry and give you a big hug, but the way things are now that just can't happen. Well I better get going now.

Sincerely,
Brandon

Assignment #11-B: Clarification Breakdown. Read Brandon's letter very carefully as if you were the victim. Circle any phrase that sounds like a thinking error (blaming, minimizing, justifying, denial, "me first," among others). Write the name of the thinking error next to it.

Assignment #11-C: In the space below, write any other reasons why Brandon's letter isn't okay.

_____
_____
_____
_____
_____
_____
_____
_____
_____
_____

If you need more space, use a separate piece of paper.

Assignment #11-D: In the space below write what's good about Brandon's letter.

_____
_____
_____
_____
_____
_____
_____
_____
_____
_____
_____
_____
_____
_____

If you need more space, use a separate piece of paper.

Assignment #11-E: Bettering Brandon. In the space below, rewrite Brandon's letter without any thinking errors. Add as many other things as you can think of to make it better.

_____

_____

_____

_____

_____

_____

_____

_____

_____

_____

_____

_____

_____

_____

_____

_____

_____

_____

If you need more space, use a separate piece of paper.

Assignment #11-F: My Clarification Letter. Now it is your turn to write a letter to each of your victims (or to their parents if your victim is a very young child). Use what you have learned so far in this chapter to help you write a detailed letter. Show the completed letter to your counselor and treatment group. They will break down your letter and identify your thinking errors and the things you may have left out, just as you broke down Brandon's letter. Rewrite your letter as many times as you have to until your group and counselor accept it. After your treatment group and your counselor have accepted the letter, copy it neatly on blank paper. **DO NOT SEND IT WITHOUT YOUR COUNSELOR'S PERMISSION!**

When the victim of your abusive behavior is a very young child, the clarification letters and meetings are often kept very short and to-the-point. Very young children sometimes can't really understand everything that has happened to them as a result of sexual abuse. When the person you abused is under 8 years old, you may be asked to write a **Future Letter**, a full clarification letter that will not be shown to the person you abused until he or she is ready to understand or needs the letter to help in therapy. If your counselor asks you to write a **Future Letter**, it will be reviewed like any other clarification letter with your group and your counselor, and then it will be kept in your counselor's files, sent to the victim's therapist, or given to the parents of the person you abused for safekeeping. **Future Letters** help child victims understand their abuse experiences when they are older and can fully understand what happened. They are just as important as clarification letters you might be allowed to send right now.

Date:_____

Dear _____:

_____
_____
_____
_____
_____
_____
_____
_____
_____
_____
_____
_____
_____
_____
_____
_____
_____
_____
_____
_____
_____
_____
_____
_____
_____
_____
_____
_____
_____

If you need more space, use a separate piece of paper.

Clarification Meetings: Talking to the Victim in Person

In clarification meetings you have an opportunity to say everything you wrote in your letter to the person you abused. Before you will be allowed to be in the same room as the victim for a clarification meeting, you must practice your presentation. Practice by using a role play with your counselor or a member of your treatment group standing in for the person you abused.

Once you have demonstrated in group that you are sensitive to the victim's feelings and have become somewhat comfortable in a role-play situation, your counselor and treatment group will give you the okay to ask permission from the victim's parents to present your clarification to them prior to meeting with the person you abused. If after seeing your presentation they agree, and the person you abused agrees, you will be allowed to present your clarification to the victim. No matter how good your presentation is, clarification meetings cannot be held unless the person you abused (and his or her counselor) gives permission. He or she has the power to set the time, place, surroundings, and the people she or he wants to be present for these meetings. The person you abused may set special conditions for you, like wanting you to stand in a corner. He or she can decide at any point not to listen any more. Often clarifications are presented over a period of time in several meetings.

Below is a list Jason made to help him remember what he wanted to say in his presentation to Jean, his stepsister:

1. Say hello and call her by name.

2. Admit that the secret touching I did was wrong, it wasn't her fault. Tell her how lucky I feel that she'll listen to me, and how good and brave she was to tell about the secret touching.

3. Tell her a little bit about what's coming in this meeting and let her know she has the choice of listening or not.

4. Say how Jean is special—that she knew I was lonely after my Dad died, and she always tried to cheer me up. Remind her about Easter at Great Aunt Betty's and that summer at the pond.

5. Say what I really did—all of it, including my grooming behaviors: First I pretended you needed help going to the bathroom. I used to take you into the bathroom and sit on the edge of the pink bathtub and watch you pee. Then I made you stay and watch me pee. That went on for about a month. Then I sat on the top stair in the hallway with the brown carpet outside your bedroom door. I would slump my shoulders and make a sad face like I was about to cry. Sometimes I would make little crying noises when I knew you were in your room. You would come out to see what was wrong, like a loving, caring sister would, and I would sit you on my lap and rock you so that your bottom was rubbing my penis through our clothes. I did that almost every week for about two months. Then I would take you into my room, pretending that you had cheered me up and we could play, and I would make up a game with the "little man" that lived inside my pants. I told you that he was really sad, too, and all droopy, but that if you would pat him and stroke him like he was a kitty cat, he would cheer up and stand up tall. And if you kept doing it, he would be so happy that he would make a fountain of vanilla syrup. I did that once a month for four months.

6. Explain that how I abused her was by taking that good quality of trying to cheer me up when I was lonely and sad and using it to do secret touching without thinking about her feelings, even though she was thinking about mine. Remind her that thinking of other people's feelings is good, and I am the one that used it in a bad way.

7. Tell some ways I think I hurt her, like that little girls should be able to turn to their big brothers for help and protection, to have fun with, like that day we made sandcastles at the beach, and how I hurt her was stealing that from her. Also I made her feel like she shouldn't care about other people's feelings. I stole the trust she should have had with my Mom (that little girls with bunnyrabbit slippers who whisper little tickles into her Mom's ear should be able to tell their moms anything or ask anything) and her Dad by making her keep secrets and telling her that they would send her away if she ever told them about the secret touching.

8. Briefly explain what I have learned about what I stole from the victim (I tried to steal the special feelings everyone has about their private parts, and the choice of who to share that with first) and why (I tried to steal that specialness because it feels really good. I was selfish and broke the rules. I tried to steal it because making you do sexual touching with me made me feel like a big important person who can boss people around. I thought only about how good I would feel, not about how bad you would feel.).

9. Tell her I care about her and that my treatment is going to help me never ignore her feelings or do secret touching again. She has a right to be mad at me for what I did.

Sometimes these person-to-person meetings are harder than the offender thinks they will be. Consider Jeff's comments after meeting with his six-year-old cousin Ryan:

> When I entered the room to face my aunt and uncle I felt like one of the lowest things on earth. I was worried about how they would react when I admitted having sexual contact with their son, Ryan. I had seen them since the incidents, but I had never talked about what I did.
>
> They looked angry, but they didn't say anything to me. When I first opened my mouth I couldn't say anything. Then I tried again. "Hello, Uncle Sean and Aunt Cora, I'm glad you are willing to listen to me talk about the sexual touching I did with Ryan last summer. I think it will really help Ryan for me to do this presentation, so he will know what really happened, how I did it, and how I am changing." They said it was okay to go ahead.
>
> I made my presentation to them. They stopped me twice and asked me to leave the room while they talked about something I said with Ryan's counselor. I was scared they were going to yell at me, but they didn't. That was almost worse. But once I realized that they weren't going to yell at me, I just wanted to do it the best I could, so they would see that Ryan deserved to hear from me in person that it wasn't his fault, it was mine, and about some of the ways he changed after I started the sexual touching. I guess I did it okay, because they told me I could meet together with them, Ryan, and Ryan's counselor.
>
> Ryan was very hyper when I came into the room. He peeked around the corner of the couch, then hid his face and told me not to look at him. I got very nervous, and looked at the wall. At first he was fidgety, but after a few minutes, he stopped. I only got to say part of my presentation the first time—it's pretty hard for a six-year-old to pay attention even to something he likes for more than 15 minutes at a time.
>
> When I was done with the first part, his counselor asked him if he was worried about me touching him again. Ryan whispered, "Yes," which made me feel even lower. My aunt told me it was important for Ryan to know I still loved him, so I told him I did, and also that I was glad he told on me and that later on, if he chose to come back to the meetings, he would hear about what I was doing to make sure I would never touch him sexually again. Another meeting was scheduled.

It took three meetings to do my whole presentation. Every time I was nervous at the beginning and relieved when it was over. Ryan asked me some questions. Sometimes I stood up, so Ryan could see how much bigger I am than him. Other times I kneeled or sat on the floor so he wouldn't feel like I was towering over him now. At the end I felt very relieved because I wasn't hiding anything anymore. And Ryan understands as much as he can about how and why I abused him. That's so important to me—because he won't grow up feeling screwed up by it as much. If he needs to talk to me when he's bigger and can understand more, that's okay with me.

Luke, an adult sex offender, also describes his meeting with his sister whom he victimized:

Meeting with Louise

At the age of 13 I started abusing my 4-year-old sister. I continued until she was 10 years old, at which time I joined the Army. Even then I abused her on every leave. The last incident happened when she was 13 years old.

Two years after I stopped abusing her Louise told someone about it and started going to counseling. Several months later it became clear to me that the state was going to prosecute me, so I entered a treatment program for sexual offenders.

The following year I received a deferred sentence on the condition that I complete a treatment program. Since that time I have been trying to face up to what I had done to her. Three years after starting treatment I finally sent a letter to Louise's counselor explaining and apologizing for the abuse. Her counselor asked if Louise wanted to read the letter, and she did. They decided to arrange a meeting between me, Louise, and both of our counselors.

As the day of the meeting approached, my counselor had a practice session where I was to talk to an empty seat, imagining that Louise was sitting there. I couldn't, but my counselor insisted. In just a few minutes the floodgates opened and my fear, embarrassment, remorse, and confusion flowed out. After avoiding and running from these feelings for years, they were finally out in the open.

The dreaded day arrived. I, with the near-perfect poker face, tough enough to handle anything, was petrified. Thoughts such as, "What if I break down in front of her?" and, "What if she's not willing to forgive me?" kept flashing through my mind. I relied on my girlfriend, Cheryl, during this time to give me support and encouragement.

On with the poker face. Calm those nerves, stop the shakes, take a deep breath, and enter the din. I was not facing the cute, defenseless girl I remembered. Oh, she was still young to me, but did not resemble the victim I remembered. After a bit I realized that she wasn't there to condemn me, not rub in my face what I had done.

She wanted to understand why I had abused her and she wanted to be sure that I was progressing in my treatment program. Her main concern was to insure the safety of her children (my nieces and nephews), as well as other children I might have contact with. However, what she wanted most was to face her own fears, which told me she was also making progress in her own treatment.

Through the years I abused her, she saw me as a grossly huge, all powerful, even evil "monster." Seeing me in person helped her to understand me as just a person, and more importantly, as someone who was no longer more powerful than her. She had faced her fears and found them to be less than she imagined.

Facing my fears, I found that she did not hate me, and was seeking to understand me. To this day we are not close. I find myself embarrassed to be with her, but it is possible to be near her at family gatherings and such. We haven't talked again about my abuse of her since the joint session, but we did exchange a letter right after the meeting.

I wish I could change the past. Since I cannot, I feel better knowing that I have taken a necessary first step toward a better future.

Assignment #11-G: What I Can Say. Now it is your turn to make a list of things you would say to the victims you abused. Give each victim's name and make a list that will help you remember key points during your person-to-person meeting. Use blank paper if you have more than one victim.

Victim's name:_____

Things to say in person-to-person meeting:

_____

_____

_____

_____

_____

_____

_____

_____

_____

_____

_____

_____

_____

_____

_____

_____

_____

_____

_____

If you need more space, use a separate piece of paper.

CHAPTER TWELVE

STEPS TO SEX-OFFENDER ACCOUNTABILITY

Now you have a basic understanding of how your offense cycle works and some idea of how you have harmed the people you abused and how you can begin making amends. These steps[1] are loosely based on the 12-step models of self-help programs such as Alcoholics Anonymous (AA). They work by giving you a deeper understanding of your offending behavior, helping you be accountable, and encouraging you to practice new behaviors that will keep you offense-free. Many sex-offender treatment programs use variations of these steps.

These steps can form a framework for your self-monitoring process during treatment and especially *afterwards* when you're more on your own. As you read them, think about what they tell you about your life. Then read them again and underneath each one write the number of the *Pathways* chapter it reminds you of. Then go on and do the assignments that go with each step.

You won't be able to finish this chapter in a week—it takes time and practice to work the steps. You may want or need to repeat some steps several times. But don't get discouraged. You're well on your way to being a member of the sexual abuse prevention team and living an offense-free life.

Steps to Sex-offender Accountability

1. Admitting I have a problem with sexual aggression and that my behavior is out of control, harmful, and irresponsible.

2. Acknowledging that I am accountable for my offenses and accepting that I need help from others.

3. Understanding how I act in irresponsible, hurtful, and criminal ways.

4. Becoming honest with others in all areas of my life.

5. Learning my offending patterns and cycles in order to understand why I choose to sexually offend.

6. Letting go of my excuses and accepting responsibility for all of my actions.

7. Understanding the consequences of my irresponsible actions for me and others.

8. Learning to feel and demonstrate remorse and empathy for those I victimized.

9. Starting to make restitution or direct amends for my crimes wherever possible.

10. Learning to have healthy and nonvictimizing relationships.

11. Continuing to act in an honest, responsible, and nonvictimizing manner to all people in my everyday life.

12. Carrying the message of accountability and responsible living to others.

---

[1]The author would like to acknowledge Jonathan Ross and Peter Loss for their early use of the 12 steps in the treatment of sexual offenders. The 12 steps in this chapter have been adapted from their work.

STEP ONE

Admitting I have a problem with sexual aggression and that my behavior is out of control, harmful, and irresponsible.

Admitting being out of control with your sexual aggression is very hard to do. At first you may not want to say that you have problems with sex. Sex offenders usually turn away from the problem and make it look like the victim is lying and crazy. The hardest thing about step one is admitting that you still have the problem, and that it did not go away after you got caught or even after treatment. The other difficult part is admitting that the problem is out of control *at this point in your process*. Most offenders would like to believe that once they have gotten into trouble, they can control their behavior without help. Few offenders are able to control their behavior by willpower alone, and many others end up reoffending over and over again. With this information in mind, complete the following assignment:

STEP 1 ASSIGNMENT

1. Write a clear statement of how your sexually abusive behavior is a problem.

_____

_____

_____

_____

_____

_____

_____

_____

_____

_____

_____

_____

_____

If you need more space, use a separate piece of paper.

2. Describe how your sexually abusive behavior is out of control.

_____

_____

_____

_____

_____
_____
_____
_____
_____
_____
_____
_____
_____

If you need more space, use a separate piece of paper.

3. Besides your counselor, admit to at least one person that you have a problem with your sexual behavior. Describe who you talked with and what they said.

_____
_____
_____
_____
_____
_____
_____
_____
_____
_____
_____
_____
_____
_____
_____
_____

If you need more space, use a separate piece of paper.

STEP TWO

Acknowledging that I am accountable for my offenses and accepting that I need help from others.

It is important to face the fact that you can't do it alone. If you try to deal with it alone, there is no one to say, "Hey, you're doing great, keep it up," or "Come on, you had best get your act together or you're going to be digging yourself a hole." Support is important, and so is having someone confront you when you are messing up. You also need to share your pain, hopelessness, happiness, and progress. Sharing these feelings is one part of this step, but you also have to be ready to accept constructive criticism. Sexual urges can be extremely strong, and you are not always strong enough to pull yourself away. You need someone to remind you about staying away from children or other victims you may be attracted to. Do your best to answer the following questions:

STEP 2 ASSIGNMENT

1. List all of your victims' first names and the number of times you sexually abused each of them:

Name   **# of Incidents**

_____

_____

_____

_____

_____

_____

_____

_____

_____

_____

If you need more space, use a separate piece of paper.

2. Describe efforts you have made thus far to stop your abusive sexual behavior:

_____

_____

_____

_____

_____

_____

_____

_____

_____

_____

_____

_____

_____

_____

If you need more space, use a separate piece of paper.

3. Describe how you tried on your own to stop your sexually abusive behavior (include thoughts you had while you were offending and things you did to control your urges):

_____

_____

_____

_____

_____

_____

_____

_____

_____

_____

_____

_____

_____

If you need more space, use a separate piece of paper.

4. List all the people in your life who are willing and able to support your efforts to control your sexual behavior (include only the people you can talk to about sexual issues):

_____

_____

_____

_____

_____

_____

_____
_____
_____
_____
_____
_____
_____

If you need more space, use a separate piece of paper.

5. Ask for and accept help in following your prevention plan from at least one person in addition to the people who have already signed your plan. Describe below what you said and what the person said in response.

_____
_____
_____
_____
_____
_____
_____
_____
_____
_____
_____
_____
_____
_____
_____
_____
_____
_____
_____

If you need more space, use a separate piece of paper.

STEP THREE

Understanding how I act in irresponsible, hurtful, and criminal ways.

This is a very important step. It is also a difficult step to face. You would rather not look at how hurtful, criminal, and irresponsible your offenses were. If you do, you'd be a jerk, a rapist, a molester, a SEX OFFENDER. But if you can't take responsibility for your actions, you need to go back to Step One and start over. It is likely that your offenses are not the only situations in which you act this way. In this step you need to look at all of the things you do that are irresponsible, hurtful, or criminal. Remember that your behavior is how you *express* who you are, but doesn't *define* who you are. Even though you have offended and acted like a jerk at times, it doesn't mean you *are* a jerk. To complete this workbook you have to believe that you can change your behavior, and be willing to do the work necessary.

STEP 3 ASSIGNMENT

1. List all of the people you have hurt in sexual ways. Describe in detail what you have done to them.

_____

_____

_____

_____

_____

_____

_____

_____

_____

_____

_____

_____

_____

_____

_____

_____

If you need more space, use a separate piece of paper.

2. List all of the people you have hurt in physical ways. Describe what you have done to hurt them.

_____

_____

_____

_____

_____

_____

_____

_____

_____

_____

_____

_____

If you need more space, use a separate piece of paper.

3. List all of the people you have hurt in a verbal or emotional way. Describe what you have said or done to hurt these people. Include all verbal harassment, name-calling, threats, etc.

_____

_____

_____

_____

_____

_____

_____

_____

_____

_____

_____

If you need more space, use a separate piece of paper.

4. Not counting the things you have already listed in this assignment, list all of the people you have hurt or affected as a result of your criminal behavior. Include all crimes that you were not caught for, as well as ones you have been caught for.

_____

_____

_____

_____

_____

_____

_____

_____

_____

_____

If you need more space, use a separate piece of paper.

5.   Get feedback from at least two adults regarding how you treat other people. Ask them what they see you doing on a daily basis that is irresponsible or hurtful. List all of their comments below.

_____

_____

_____

_____

_____

_____

_____

_____

_____

_____

_____

_____

_____

_____

_____

_____

_____

_____

_____

_____

If you need more space, use a separate piece of paper.

STEP FOUR

Becoming honest with others in all areas of my life.

Going back to the people you lied to is hard—you probably never thought of doing it before you got into a treatment program. Begin by making a list of everyone you lied to about your sexual behavior. Then start writing letters to those people explaining exactly what you really did and what you are doing to get help for your problems. Your list probably will include people like your probation officer, lawyer, relatives, counselors, or even judges. Some people who receive the letters will have a negative reaction. Some people may want you prosecuted. Normally, though, people tend to develop respect for offenders who take the risk of telling the truth about their offenses. Below is an example of such a letter:

Dear Mr. Johnson:

My name is Billy Smith and you were my probation officer six months ago when I went to court for an indecent liberties charge. When I talked with you back then I told you I did not do my offenses. Since then I've been in treatment and I have admitted to raping all three victims. I want you to know that I am getting help for my problems, and I just wanted to set the record straight because my lies were bothering me. I am working on being an honest person, and I will keep working hard so I won't hurt anybody else. Thank you for listening to me.

Sincerely,
Billy Smith

STEP 4 ASSIGNMENT

1. Make a list of everybody you have lied to about your sexual behavior.

_____

_____

_____

_____

_____

_____

_____

If you need more space, use a separate piece of paper.

2. List everybody you have been *totally honest* with regarding your sexual offenses. "Totally honest" means no thinking errors.

_____

_____

_____

_____

_____

_____

_____

_____

If you need more space, use a separate piece of paper.

3. Write a sample letter in the space below to one of the people on your list of people you have lied to. The letter should include an admission of your dishonesty, an explanation of what the truth really was, and a description of what you are doing in treatment. After the letter is approved by your group or counselor, you may be asked to recopy the letter on clean paper in order to send it to the person.

Dear _____ :

_____

_____

_____

_____

_____

_____

_____

_____

_____

_____

If you need more space, use a separate piece of paper.

4. Make a plan for correcting your lies to the people you listed under #1. The plan could include face-to-face discussion so you can tell the whole truth about what you did, or could involve phone calls and letters describing what really happened. Include a completion date for each activity with each person.

Person	Plan	Completion Date

If you need more space, use a separate piece of paper.

5. Now describe other things in your life that you have a hard time being honest about. It could be anything—having been sexually abused, using drugs, stealing, joyriding, grades, relationships, etc.

_____

_____

_____

_____

_____

_____

_____

_____

_____

_____

_____

_____

If you need more space, use a separate piece of paper.

6. Make a plan for becoming an honest person in your day-to-day life. For example, explain how you can stop lying and start telling the whole truth without using "thinking errors."

_____

_____

_____

_____

_____

_____

_____

_____

_____

_____

_____

_____

_____

_____

_____

If you need more space, use a separate piece of paper.

STEP FIVE

Learning my offending patterns and cycles in order to understand why I choose to sexually offend.

This step will help you learn more about the life-needs you met by committing sexual offenses. It will also help you understand why you continued to commit sexual offenses after you knew they were wrong, hurtful, and dangerous.

You will also need to learn about something called *gratification*. *Gratification* means getting something you want or desire. People often use drugs, sex, food, or alcohol for their immediate (right now) gratification because they can't deal with getting what they *really* want—a better job, a serious relationship, a diploma or a degree, maybe even just a hug or a pat on the back for a job well done. During this treatment process you will need to learn how to postpone gratification, to put it off until a more appropriate time with a more appropriate goal. Remember the old song, "You can't always get what you want"? Well, it's true, and these exercises will help you learn to postpone gratification and learn to make better choices about how to get what you *really* want.

STEP 5 ASSIGNMENT

1. Make a list of all the problems you were having before your offenses began (For example: failing at school, fighting with parents, no friends, using drugs, feeling lonely, breaking the law, etc.)

_____

_____

_____

_____

_____

_____

_____

_____

_____

_____

If you need more space, use a separate piece of paper.

2. Describe how you were thinking and feeling about things that were happening to you in your life before your offenses began.

_____

_____

_____

_____

_____

_____

_____

_____

_____

If you need more space, use a separate piece of paper.

3. How did you think and feel before, during, and after your offenses?

_____

_____

_____

_____

_____

_____

_____

_____

_____

If you need more space, use a separate piece of paper.

4. Describe how your offending pattern might have been a type of cycle. Explain how your activities, thoughts, and feelings before your offenses helped to contribute to your choice to offend. Also describe how your feelings during and after the offenses led you on to more offenses.

_____

_____

_____

_____

_____

_____

_____

_____

_____

If you need more space, use a separate piece of paper.

5. List all of the benefits you got from your sexual offenses (for example, satisfaction, revenge, orgasm, a good sexual feeling, envy by peers, etc.):

_____

_____

_____

_____

_____

_____

_____

_____

_____

6. Now list all of the costs you incurred from your sexual offenses (for example, lost job, friends, criminal record, family rejected me, etc.):

_____

_____

_____

_____

_____

_____

_____

_____

_____

7. Now compare the two—benefits and costs. Which list is longer?

_____

_____

_____

_____

_____

_____

_____

STEP SIX

Letting go of my excuses and accepting responsibility for all of my actions.

This step may seem easy but it is really very hard to accomplish. By now you have learned to throw away your excuses for your offenses and clearly say, "I did choose to offend." The key part of this step is "*all* of my actions," which means you have to be responsible in *all* of your day-to-day actions. This is hard for anybody. This assignment will help you get on the right path.

STEP 6 ASSIGNMENT

1. List all of the excuses you have used to explain why you committed your offenses:

_____

_____

_____

_____

_____

_____

_____

_____

_____

_____

_____

_____

If you need more space, use a separate piece of paper.

2. Now write "I chose to offend sexually" 10 times below:

_____

_____

_____

_____

_____

_____

_____

_____

_____

_____

3. Make a list of your other behaviors or problems for which you sometimes have difficulty taking responsibility:

_____

_____

_____

_____

_____

_____

_____

_____

_____

_____

If you need more space, use a separate piece of paper.

4. List at least five examples of times you have taken responsibility this week for your actions rather than making up excuses.

_____

_____

_____

_____

_____

_____

_____

_____

_____

_____

_____

_____

_____

_____

_____

_____

If you need more space, use a separate piece of paper.

STEP SEVEN

Understanding the consequences of my irresponsible actions for me and others.

In this step the goal is to learn how your irresponsible actions have consequences for yourself and others. Don't get caught up in self-pity over your consequences; instead, begin to appreciate how your behavior affects others.

STEP 7 ASSIGNMENT

1. Make a list of how your sex offenses affected others (victims, victim's family, friends, community, etc.). Focus on the impact your behavior has had on others, not on the impact your behavior has had on you.

_____

_____

_____

_____

_____

_____

_____

_____

_____

If you need more space, use a separate piece of paper.

2. Describe how your sex offenses affected you. Think of all the consequences of your actions, not just your court sentence. For example, think of the emotional consequences of your offenses (e.g. rejection by others, lack of trust, suspicion, reputation, labels, name-calling, etc.). How does it feel to be a sex offender?

_____

_____

_____

_____

_____

_____

_____

_____

If you need more space, use a separate piece of paper.

STEP EIGHT

Learning to feel and demonstrate remorse and empathy for those I victimized.

Remorse is a feeling you have when you truly and sincerely regret something you did. In order to feel empathy for the person you abused, you have to really know and understand what it is like for the other person. True empathy is hard to develop, especially when you sometimes don't care about yourself.

STEP 8 ASSIGNMENT

1. Describe a time in your life when you felt hurt, alone, betrayed, or powerless. Include details about what happened.

_____

_____

_____

_____

_____

_____

_____

_____

_____

_____

_____

_____

If you need more space, use a separate piece of paper.

2. How did you feel at the time, and how did you show your feelings?

_____

_____

_____

_____

_____

_____

_____

_____

_____

If you need more space, use a separate piece of paper.

3. Read the following victim perspective assignment that was done by Peter near the end of his treatment process.

It was two o'clock on a Monday afternoon. I was sitting in class and dreading the end of the school day. I knew that my older brother Peter would be home and waiting for me. I didn't want to go home, I knew what would happen. I would come home and call my mom right away to tell her I was home. What I really wanted was to tell her that I didn't want to be alone with Peter and also tell her about what he was doing to me. Now I really didn't want to go home. All he's going to do is put on that nasty movie and start undressing himself and me. And then he'd — I don't even want to think about what he'd do next!

Then the bell rang — loud and heavy as if it knew what would happen next. I was the last one to leave the room, I looked around dreadfully frightened. The teacher smiled at me and waved good-bye. Then she got up all of a sudden and started walking towards me. She asked me if there was anything wrong? "Oh-no, nothing," I lied. Then she said "You'd better hurry or else you'll be late for your bus." Well good-bye! I smiled and left the room, closing the door behind me. I walked with heavy footsteps down the corridor towards the door. I got on the bus with heavy thoughts and the bus driver pulled away. Fifteen minutes later the bus pulled up to my stop. I got up and looked out the window. The bus driver yelled in a firm voice, "Come on, this is your stop." I walked towards the front of the bus and down the steps. The door slammed heavily behind me and I started walking up the street towards my house trying to see if my brother was in fact there, hoping against all hope that he wasn't. I couldn't tell either way, so I walked up the stairs and tried the lock — it was open!

Oh, no — he's home. I gathered up all my courage and opened the door. I could hear his music but he was nowhere in sight. I closed the door very lightly behind and tiptoed to my room so as not to let him know that I'm home. I got to my room and closed that door too! Oh, how I always wished that it had a lock so I could lock him out. I picked up the phone and dialed to mom's work. "Yes, can I speak to Molly please? Thank you." I talked to my mom for about five minutes and then she had to go. I sat alone in my room doing my homework for about an hour undisturbed. I almost thought that he'd leave me alone today, but then...

I heard footsteps coming up the stairs and towards my room. I made myself busy doing homework, hoping that he'd leave me alone for once. The door opened and in came my brother. I did not look around, I just heard him come in and sit down on my bed. I still didn't make a sound, just sitting there writing very fast and then my pencil broke. Oh, no. I put the pencil into the pencil sharpener and heard him get up and say "What are you doing?" "Can't you see you big bully that I'm doing my homework like I should?" I thought to myself. "Nothing," I grumbled at him. "Wanna come out and watch the movie with me?" "No, is that all he can think about?" I thought. "Oh, come on," he begged me. I got up knowing that nothing will help anyway and walked out behind him into the living room. I sat down on the couch and he turned the ugly movie on. He sat down next to me and watched the movie for a little while, then his hand came over to my pants and started to unbutton them. He pulled my pants off of me and slid his fingers into my underwear. "Why does he have to keep doing this to me?" That kind of tickles, but it's so bad I don't want him to do this to me.

"What are you doing?" I asked even though I knew when he pulled my underwear down and slid his head between my legs. He didn't answer, how typical of him. He put his face right up to my crotch and looked at me. I looked away. Then he started to lick my privates. Although that did feel kind of good, I still hated every moment of it. He kept licking my privates and moving his penis up and down with his hand. I looked at the T.V. and asked him "Why are they doing that?" and he said "Because they like it." Finally he started doing that thing to his penis a lot faster and licking my privates harder and then he stopped finally. He got up, turned off the T.V., and got dressed, not even asking how I felt. I wish he'd stop doing this once and for all. I picked up my clothing and went into the bathroom. When I got out I knew that he wouldn't bother me no more today — thank God, it's over. I went into my room and finished my homework. He made some sandwiches for the both of us and brought them into my room. He said, "I'm sorry and I promise I won't do that to you anymore." I knew that was a lie though but he did leave me alone for a couple of weeks. He must have heard me crying in the bathroom.

4. Directions: Now it is your turn to put yourself in the role of a victim and try to describe an experience you put a victim through during your abusive behavior. If your counselor approves, you may also describe a personal sexual abuse experience you have gone through as part of this assignment. The idea is to recreate the setting, experience, and emotions so you can better understand a victim's experience. First fill out the information requested. Then describe how the victim felt when she or he was being groomed and the victim's thoughts and feelings while the abuse was happening. Use the "first person" ("I feel," "hurts me") to do this assignment and describe it as if it is happening to you right now. It might look something like: "He is pulling my underwear down, his hand is cold. What is he doing to me?" Try to use words the victim would actually use. If you are doing this assignment about your own abuse, try to describe what you thought and what your feelings were about the abuse when it was happening. Use as many extra pages as you need for this assignment.

Victim's name: _____

Abuser's name: _____

Victim's age at time of offense: _____

Offender's age at time of offense: _____

Approximate date of offense: _____

Location of offense:_____

Start here with the story:

_____

_____

_____

If you need more space, use a separate piece of paper.

STEP NINE

Starting to make restitution or direct amends for my crimes wherever possible.

In this step you start to mend the harm you've caused. Sometimes this is hard because many offenders want to believe that they have already paid the price in getting caught and going through treatment, detention, or jail. The goal here is to start to work to make things better for the people you abused directly, or other victims indirectly. Start with any victims with whom you have not already gone through the clarification process (reread *Pathways* Chapters Four, Nine, and Ten to remind yourself of ways to be sensitive to victims' feelings).

STEP 9 ASSIGNMENT

1. Make a list of people you have hurt with your sexual offending behavior.

_____

_____

_____

_____

_____

_____

_____

_____

If you need more space, use a separate piece of paper.

2. Develop a plan to make direct amends to every person you have hurt. List the person, the plan, and the dates you started and finished.

Person	Plan	Start Date	Finish Date

If you need more space, use a separate piece of paper.

3. Discuss these plans with your counselor or probation/parole officer. In the space below describe his/her response. Modify the plans as necessary, then, with permission from your counselor or probation/parole officer, contact each person on the list to carry out the plan. ***Remember, do not contact the people you abused without permission from their counselors or parents!***

_____

_____

_____

_____

_____

_____

_____

_____

_____

_____

_____

_____

_____

_____

_____

_____

_____

_____

_____

_____

_____

_____

_____

_____

_____

_____

_____

_____

If you need more space, use a separate piece of paper.

STEP TEN

Learning to have healthy and nonvictimizing relationships.

In this step you have to work toward building relationships that are equal, caring, loving, and consenting. This is hard because many offenders have not experienced these types of relationships. This assignment will help you look at this issue.

STEP 10 ASSIGNMENT

1. For you, what is a healthy and appropriate relationship?

_____

_____

_____

_____

_____

_____

_____

If you need more space, use a separate piece of paper.

2. How can you tell if a relationship is healthy?

_____

_____

_____

_____

_____

_____

_____

_____

If you need more space, use a separate piece of paper.

3. What qualities are you looking for in a partner for a sexual relationship?

_____

_____

_____

_____

_____

_____

_____

_____

_____

If you need more space, use a separate piece of paper.

4. What relationships are you involved in now that you would describe as healthy? Include all friendships.

_____

_____

_____

_____

_____

_____

_____

_____

If you need more space, use a separate piece of paper.

5. What relationships are you involved in now that you would describe as unhealthy? List the reason as well (for example, lying, keeping secrets, the person uses me, etc.).

Person   **Reason**

_____

_____

_____

_____

_____

_____

_____

_____

If you need more space, use a separate piece of paper.

6. How would you talk with a sexual partner about birth control and sexually transmitted diseases? Describe exactly what you would say.

_____

_____

_____

_____

_____

_____

_____

_____

_____

_____

_____

_____

If you need more space, use a separate piece of paper.

7. List 10 things you can do to make sure that all your relationships are healthy and appropriate.

1. _____

2. _____

3. _____

4. _____

5. _____

6. _____

7. _____

8. _____

9. _____

10. _____

STEP ELEVEN

Continuing to act in an honest, responsible, and nonvictimizing
manner to all people in my everyday life.

Nobody expects perfection, just honesty and responsibility. This means telling the truth *all* the time, following through on expectations, rules, and basic day-to-day necessities. It also means not expecting others to baby you. The following assignment is a starting point.

STEP 11 ASSIGNMENT

1. Describe how you act in an honest, responsible, and nonvictimizing way in your everyday life.

_____

_____

_____

_____

_____

_____

_____

_____

If you need more space, use a separate piece of paper.

2. Describe the ways in which you do *not* act in an honest, responsible, and nonvictimizing way in your everyday life.

_____

_____

_____

_____

_____

_____

_____

_____

If you need more space, use a separate piece of paper.

3. Ask at least two adults you know well for feedback about what you wrote in #1 and #2 above. Write their feedback below and have them sign the sheet indicating they said what you wrote.

Adult #1:_____

_____

_____

_____

_____

_____

_____

_____

_____

Signature:_____

Adult #2:_____

_____

_____

_____

_____

_____

_____

_____

_____

Signature:_____

4. How can you decide who to tell about your past sexual behavior? Teenagers with sexual behavior problems usually would prefer that nobody else find out about it. But building a support system and being honest about past problems is one of your treatment goals while working in *Pathways*. On the other hand there are some risks for you as a teenager in telling others about your past sexual problems. If you tell a close friend, there is always a risk that if the friendship ends badly, the person will tell others the private information you have shared in order to get revenge or to feel more powerful than you. Teenagers often see things in all-or-nothing ways: things and people seem either all good or all bad. They may react to knowing that you have had sexual behavior problems by dropping you as a friend because they can no longer see beyond the hurtful behavior to what's good in you. How can you balance out these concerns?

In *Pathways* you have been encouraged to practice honesty and responsible behavior. Based on the experience of hundreds of teenage sex offenders, it usually works best to be honest and tell a potential sexual partner about your past behavior problems *before* you start a sexual relationship. This doesn't mean telling every new girlfriend or boyfriend right away about your history. But you should probably say something about your sexual offending behaviors and issues *before* you get involved in any sexual behavior. If your relationship is based on good friendship, where there is caring, love, support, trust, and honesty, it will survive this storm. A good rule to remember is that if you're not ready to share your story with a potential sexual partner, you're probably not ready to have sex in that relationship, either. Many teenage sex offenders have learned the hard way about telling a sexual partner about their past sexual offending behavior *after* they had already been sexual. Their partners felt betrayed and misled, and many ended their relationships.

But what if you tell your partner and she or he doesn't want to have a sexual relationship with you any more? Well, this is the real world, and every partner should have that choice. That is what *consent* means: having all the facts and making an informed choice. Now the good news! The majority of teenaged sex offenders find that their closest friends and partners respond with *increased* care and affection when the offenders take such a huge risk and tell about their sexual offense histories. Any relationship you lose because you've been honest about your past behavior probably wouldn't have lasted. Honesty pays off in relationship strength and stability and in self-respect.

Which friends have you told about your sexual behavior problems? How did they react? List their names and reactions below.

1. _____

Reaction: _____

_____

_____

2. _____

Reaction: _____

_____

_____

3. _____

Reaction: _____

_____

_____

STEP TWELVE

Carrying the message of accountability and responsible living to others.

This step is as much for you as it is for others. While it does feel good to help yourself, this step is also about helping others. Sexual abuse is a huge problem in our society, and efforts need to be made to deal with the problem in a better way. Since you have contributed to the problem in a negative way, it is time that you take a positive step and do something to help others. There are many different ways to do this. In the assignment below you will be given several different options.

STEP 12 ASSIGNMENT

1.   Review each of the 12 steps. List one important thing you learned from each step.

Step 1:_____

_____

Step 2:_____

_____

Step 3:_____

_____

Step 4:_____

_____

Step 5:_____

_____

Step 6:_____

_____

Step 7:_____

_____

Step 8:_____

_____

Step 9:_____

_____

Step 10:_____

_____

Step 11:_____

_____

Step 12:_____

_____

2. Choose someone to talk to about what you have learned about the steps to accountability. If possible, the person should be another teenage sex offender who is just starting treatment. If this is not possible, share the information with an adult in your life.

The person you have chosen is:_____

Date information shared:_____

Person's signature:_____

3. Sometimes teenage sex offenders can share what they have learned in treatment with the public as a way of getting the message to others that some sex offenders are serious about treatment and accountability. Consider this letter written by a teenage sex offender to the editor of a major newspaper as a way of carrying the message of accountability to others.

Dear Editor:

I am a 16-year-old male sex offender currently under treatment with the S.S.O.D.A. program, an outpatient treatment program for teenage sex offenders. I have been in the program for over a year, and would like to share with you and others some things I feel are important to know about sex offenders and this program.

I was sentenced and placed in this program two summers ago, for twice sexually victimizing a young girl. During the time that I was in treatment I learned much about my behaviors and ways of thinking that lead up to my offending. I've learned a lot about how I have hurt the person I abused, her family, and my own family. I have seen through treatment that sex offending isn't simply a one-time occurrence. It is a continuous cycle that can carry on for years. The initial offense can start a chain reaction. I believe that somewhere there has to be a break in this cycle or it can go on for years. I was fortunate that the girl I abused was brave enough to tell someone about what I did. If she didn't have that courage, I probably would have never been caught, and neither of us would have received help to deal with what I had done. I would have continued to offend against people, and the child I abused may have had any number of behavior problems. Because the child spoke out, we are both getting the help we need. I am hopeful that I will not offend again, and that the child will eventually recover from the abuse I put her through.

I understand why most people are not supportive of sex offenders. I imagine that many people would prefer to have us locked away forever. What we did *was* horrible. But many of us really want to learn how not to behave in this way, how not to hurt people, and we *can* learn to overcome our problem with hard work and our real desire to get better.

Another thing that can be done to help is to listen to your children. If they tell you that someone has been hurting them or doing bad touching, be sure you listen to them. I've never met another sex offender who would have admitted to their offenses without being caught, and many continue to deny their offenses after someone confronts them. Someone else finding out about the offense is the first step towards treatment. Not all offenders are treatable, either. Many are sent to jails or receive institutional treatment instead of outpatient treatment. Most of us who have received the S.S.O.D.A. program consider ourselves very fortunate to have such an opportunity. We also have to work hard to stay in treatment, and our privilege can be revoked quite easily if we fail to do our part.

I would like to thank you for taking the time to read my letter. I hope it has provided some insight about sex offenders.

Felix W.H.

Write your own letter to the editor describing what you have learned in treatment. You do not have to send the letter unless *you* decide to send it.

Dear Editor:

_____

_____

_____

_____

_____

_____

_____

_____

_____

_____

_____

_____

_____

_____

_____

_____

_____

_____

_____

_____

_____

_____

_____

_____

If you need more space, use a separate piece of paper.

CHAPTER THIRTEEN

HOW AM I DOING? A NEW ATTITUDE

Now that you are nearing the end of *Pathways* you may be feeling somewhat confident that your problem is under control and that you will never reoffend. Unfortunately, treatment is not that simple; if it were, there would be far fewer adult sex offenders today. Remember the three stages of denial you learned about in Chapter Three? The third stage of denial is *denial of the continuing problem.* In order to keep yourself safe and prevent yourself from reoffending, you will need to look at *all* your personality traits and work to develop a responsible and healthy set of values, attitudes, and behaviors. Listen to what happened to Philip, a 14-year-old offender who had been in treatment for several months:

> I was just picked up by my father outside of the big department store in the mall. I was caught for shoplifting. It was purely a lack of judgement, especially when in my mind I knew if I were to get caught it would perhaps result in detention. My judgement is obviously extremely bad. Is it really difficult at all to determine if something is wrong or right?
>
> I feel especially ashamed towards my parents. They have helped me through treatment and the whole thing with my sexual assault of Jeremy. They allowed themselves to regain their trust in me, but I cannot see how they will ever be able to trust me again. I have decided that from this point on I will need to be a much more responsible person in the sense that however slight of an action I am doing or involved in, I must first study the consequences in my mind and in that sense use better judgement.

Philip learned the hard way that his sexual problem was not separate from the rest of his problems. He had been having problems for years getting along with others, and he had become very self-centered and impulsive. If he *wanted* something, he *had* to have it, no matter what the consequences were. When it came to his sexual problem, he knew it was wrong, but decided he wanted to do it anyway. It was useless to try to help him change his sexual problem without helping him change his everyday behavior.

Like Philip, you may have urges to act out in both sexual and nonsexual ways. If you have done your work in *Pathways* well, you now have some tools to help you handle these urges and change your behaviors and the attitudes that maintain them. You're not done with working on yourself, even though you're almost done with this workbook. The rest is up to you. Read your warning signs every day. Put your Offense Prevention Plans into action. Work the 12 Steps. Practice being honest with yourself and everyone else in your life.

Assignment #13-A: Building up My Reoffense Barriers. One of your final assignments in *Pathways* is to complete the reoffense barrier chart that follows. Your job is to build up each barrier as high as you can, using all of the knowledge you have gained in your treatment and in completing this workbook. You may want to review Chapters Five through Nine. This is your opportunity to "put it all together." Remember it takes only one barrier to prevent a reoffense, but the stronger all of them are, the less your chances of reoffending.

BUILDING UP MY REOFFENSE BARRIERS

Motivation	Internal Barriers	External Barriers	Victim Resistance
_____	_____	_____	_____
_____	_____	_____	_____
_____	_____	_____	_____
_____	_____	_____	_____
_____	_____	_____	_____
_____	_____	_____	_____
_____	_____	_____	_____
_____	_____	_____	_____
_____	_____	_____	_____
_____	_____	_____	_____
_____	_____	_____	_____
_____	_____	_____	_____
_____	_____	_____	_____
_____	_____	_____	_____
_____	_____	_____	_____
_____	_____	_____	_____
_____	_____	_____	_____

Example:

Practice healthy, consenting fantasies	Think about how my victims have been hurt	No babysitting	Completing my clarification letters

Assignment #13-B: How Am I Doing? The next assignment for this chapter is to complete the following questionnaire. It will test your attitudes and knowledge about sexual offending. Your answers should reflect the information you have gained through completing this workbook. Your counselor may have had you complete this questionnaire at the beginning of your treatment or during evaluation, so this is a chance to show what you have learned since then. Good luck, and remember to answer honestly!

ADOLESCENT SEXUAL INFORMATION SCALE

Read carefully each of the statements below. Circle the number next to each statement that best describes your personal response to it.

		Strongly Agree	Agree Some	Neutral	Disagree Some	Strongly Disagree
1.	When you really think about it, most victims of sexual abuse didn't do anything to cause the abuse to happen.	1	2	3	4	5
2.	If other people sexually touch or rub strangers on the bus, then it is okay for me to do it too.	1	2	3	4	5
3.	Very young children can make their own decisions about whether they want to have sex with me or not.	1	2	3	4	5
4.	Taking someone's underwear, feeling it or wearing it for sexual purposes would be dangerous for me to do.	1	2	3	4	5
5.	Everyone should expect to be sexually hurt or abused sometime during their life.	1	2	3	4	5
6.	Masturbation is okay to do, even for sex offenders.	1	2	3	4	5
7.	A sexual act can only be called rape if the person tries to fight back the entire time.	1	2	3	4	5
8.	If I just look through the windows at somebody, it can't hurt anyone.	1	2	3	4	5
9.	It is not very likely that I can pick up a stranger on the bus by rubbing her body and touching her.	1	2	3	4	5
10.	If a child doesn't tell anyone about having sex with me, then he/she really liked it.	1	2	3	4	5

	Strongly Agree	Agree Some	Neutral	Disagree Some	Strongly Disagree
11. Some people are so shy about asking for sex that they really want you to force sex on them.	1	2	3	4	5
12. Most sex offenders would be better off by talking about their sexual behavior and admitting everything they've done.	1	2	3	4	5
13. Rape is so common now that most people are not upset by being raped.	1	2	3	4	5
14. If someone stares at my private parts while I'm exposing myself, it means that person really enjoys looking at them.	1	2	3	4	5
15. A child would never have sex with me unless he/she really wanted to.	1	2	3	4	5
16. There are some situations where sexually hurting someone is okay.	1	2	3	4	5
17. If someone says "no" to me sexually, it usually means no.	1	2	3	4	5
18. There is effective treatment for a person who commits sex crimes.	1	2	3	4	5
19. Most sexual offenses with children are caused by the child acting sexy around the older person.	1	2	3	4	5
20. Persons accused of sex crimes shouldn't tell anybody about what they've done.	1	2	3	4	5
21. Children are harmed only when offenders use force to make them have sex with them.	1	2	3	4	5

	Strongly Agree	Agree Some	Neutral	Disagree Some	Strongly Disagree
22. If I expose myself to someone, it is likely that person will want to have sex with me afterwards.	1	2	3	4	5
23. Most adult sex offenders begin their sexual offending as teenagers.	1	2	3	4	5
24. Sex offenses are caused by the offender's own experience as a victim of sexual abuse.	1	2	3	4	5
25. Children often lie by making up stories of sexual abuse.	1	2	3	4	5

To find out how you did on this test, ask your counselor to score your answers and discuss with you what your scores mean.

Assignment #13-C: Freedom from Offending Contract. This contract is a way for you to plan the next several years after you finish treatment. Now that you have worked through *Pathways*, it is time for you to use what you have learned on your own. Fill out this contract form, and then share it with your parents, counselor, treatment group, foster parent, group home staff, or your closest friends. The idea is that the people around you will have some idea of the restrictions and rules that you plan to live with once you are out of treatment and off probation or parole.

Personal FFO (Freedom From Offending) Contract

1. **Personal Information:**

   Name: _____ Date: _____

   Date you started treatment:_____

   Date of planned graduation from treatment:_____

   Your age now:_____

2. **Sexual Offense History:**

   A. Sex and general age range of the people you have admitted abusing: _____

   _____

   _____

   B. Specific sexual acts: what exactly did you do to the people you abused? You may combine all acts performed with different victims:_____

   _____

   _____

   _____

   _____

   _____

   C. Assault process: describe *how* you committed your offenses, such as the type of force, bribes, games, etc., you used: _____

   _____

   _____

   _____

   _____

   _____

3. **Description of your offending cycles:**

   A. Describe the thoughts and thinking errors that you might have at the beginning of your offending or maintenance cycles. For example, "It's hopeless, nobody cares, I'm a bad person," etc.

   _____

   _____

   _____

   _____

   _____

   _____

   _____

   B. Describe the feelings that you might have when you are entering your cycle. For example: "I feel angry, mad, lonely, bored, rejected, worthless, disappointed," etc.

   _____

   _____

   _____

   _____

   _____

   _____

   _____

   _____

   C. What behaviors might you do when you are getting into your cycle? For example: "I use drugs, I isolate myself, I pick fights, I talk about sex a lot," etc.

   _____

   _____

   _____

   _____

   _____

   _____

   _____

4. **Description of how your cycle affects your life:**

A. Social life: How do your relationships with your family and friends change as you go into your deviant cycle? For example, "I stop going out with friends. I stop telling my parents where I'm going. I stop calling my friends. I close my family out of my life," etc.

_____

_____

_____

_____

_____

_____

B. School: If you go to school, describe how your school performance changes when you are in your deviant cycle or a maintenance cycle. For example: "I cut classes, my grades go down, I don't do homework, I get kicked out of class," etc.

_____

_____

_____

_____

_____

_____

C. Work: If you work, describe how your work behavior changes when you are in your deviant cycle or a maintenance cycle. For example: "I skip work, I stop caring about the job I'm doing, I go to work high, I steal from my job," etc.

_____

_____

_____

_____

_____

_____

_____

D. Appearance: Describe how your personal grooming and appearance changes when you are in your deviant cycle or a maintenance cycle. For example, "I don't shower, I wear the same clothes all the time, I look tired, my hair gets long and shaggy, I don't shave," etc.

_____

_____

_____

_____

_____

_____

E. Home: Describe how your home life changes when you are in your deviant cycle or a maintenance cycle. For example, "I get sloppy, I don't pick up my messes, I argue about doing my chores, I watch TV instead of doing sports or riding my bike or doing homework," etc.

_____

_____

_____

_____

_____

_____

5. **Long-Term Environmental Restrictions:**

Your long-term success will depend to a large extent on the long-term personal boundaries and barriers you build into your life after treatment. List your plan for keeping up your barriers after you leave treatment. Be realistic.

A. Contact with children: under what circumstances will you let yourself have contact with children more than three years younger than yourself?

_____

_____

_____

_____

_____

_____

_____

B. Drugs or alcohol: under what circumstances will you let yourself engage in drug or alcohol use? How do you intend to keep it from being a problem?

_____

_____

_____

_____

_____

_____

_____

_____

C. Knowledge of your history of offending: who will you tell in the future about your history of sexual offenses? Why or why not?

_____

_____

_____

_____

_____

_____

_____

D. Sex life: what role will sex play in your future relationships? How do you intend to keep the sexual element of your relationships healthy and responsible?

_____

_____

_____

_____

_____

_____

_____

E. Work: what jobs do you hope to pursue in the future? What jobs will you put off-limits for yourself based on your history?

_____

_____

_____

_____

_____

_____

_____

_____

6. Alternatives to Offending:

What will you do, who will you call to prevent yourself from reoffending when you find yourself in your offense cycle or in a high risk situation?

_____

_____

_____

_____

_____

_____

_____

_____

7. Positive Self-Esteem Building:

Make a list of all the positive, healthy activities you plan to be involved in during the two years following treatment.

_____

_____

_____

_____

_____

_____

_____

8. Long-Term Goals:

Describe what you hope to achieve during the next three years. Be as specific as you can. Include school, work, family, health, and relationship goals, etc.

School: _____

_____

_____

_____

_____

Work: _____

_____

_____

_____

_____

Family: _____

_____

_____

_____

_____

Health: _____

_____

_____

_____

_____

Relationships: _____

_____

_____

_____

_____

If you need more space, use a separate piece of paper.

ENDNOTE: THE PATH CONTINUES

Congratulations on your successful completion of *Pathways*. Your work has taken many hours of your time. You should have a clearer understanding of your offending cycle, as well as knowledge of how you can reduce your long-term risk of reoffending. Remember, completing *Pathways* does not mean that you are cured. It does mean that with continued attention, you can control your behavior so that you never offend again. While some teenage sex offenders go on to become adult sex offenders, many do not. In completing all of your *Pathways* assignments, you have learned that overcoming sexual offending patterns is not easy. It takes continued hard work, support, and major lifestyle changes.

Don't hesitate to ask for help if you find yourself slipping back into your offending cycle. You have learned that you must stay out of situations that give you opportunities to offend. The better able you are to make these kinds of changes, the more likely you are to remain offense-free. Completing *Pathways* does *not* mean that your treatment is over. While many of you are well on your way toward transition from treatment to aftercare and self-monitoring, completion of this workbook is only one step is that direction. To be successful as a member of the sexual abuse prevention team, you must go out and practice in your everyday life what you have learned in treatment.

Kevin, a teenage sex offender, wrote about his treatment process at the time of his transition from a treatment program into aftercare:

> The greatest impact that treatment had on my life was the actual changing of my abusive behavior, such as needing to have the last word or having a feeling that it was necessary to put down someone I disliked.
>
> I feel treatment was a very successful point in my life because of the hard work I put into it. It also gave me the ability to have feelings of empathy for my victims, because of what I learned about just what happens to someone who is victimized. I feel that had I not gone through the treatment program as I did, I would have been no different than a monster who goes around offending children. I am grateful to that person who turned me in because that gave me a way to express all of the feelings that had built up inside of me.

Remember Kim, the young woman whose words you read in Chapter One? She has more to say:

> When I started *Pathways* I was 13 years old. Now, as I write this, I am 14 years old. Now that you have finished *Pathways* you are prepared for what lies ahead. You know how to respond to your emotions and physical feelings in a positive way. Don't think that you are free from court, rules, and your problem forever. Think positive about yourself. What you did was wrong, but don't let it get the best of you. I am making a plan for my next five years that keeps me in a safer position and builds up my integrity. I hope that you make a plan too, so that you don't let yourself fall back into negative cycles or old habits. As you leave *Pathways*, practice all that you have learned. Don't go back to taking joyrides and being self-centered. I have been abused, and I have abused. I am going to do whatever it takes to never hurt another person. And I want that for you too.

If you have successfully completed *Pathways*, you deserve recognition. You are making an honest effort to control your abusive sexual behavior. As you continue along the path to prevention and safety, remember you are not alone. You have the support of many people who care about you, including all of the people in your personal support system. Believe in yourself, work hard, and always remember that the key to prevention and safety is in maintaining the healthy lifestyle changes that help you feel good about who you are. Remember, it is up to you to make the choices in your life that will make your treatment successful. Always be prepared for the possibility of an offense occurring, because you will then be ready to turn to your Prevention Plan to stop the abusive behavior before it happens again.

Good luck with everything you do in your life to become and remain a caring, responsible, and nonoffending person.

RECOMMENDED READINGS

Most of the books on this list are available at your local bookstore. A few are available only by writing to the publisher at the address given.

Young, Gay & Proud! edited by Sasha Alyson (1985). Alyson Publications, P.O. Box 2783 Dept. B-1, Boston, MA 02208.

Macho! Is That What I Really Want? by Py Bateman & Bill Mahoney (1986). Youth Education Systems, Box 223, Scarborough, NY 10510. $4.75.

The Me Nobody Knows: A Guide for Teen Survivors by Barbara Bean and Shari Bennett (1993). Lexington Books/Macmillian, New York, NY.

Adults Molested As Children: A Survivor's Manual For Women & Men by Euan Bear with Peter Dimock (1988). Safer Society Press, P.O. Box 340, Brandon, VT 05733-0340.

Changing Bodies, Changing Lives: A Book for Teens on Sex and Relationships by Ruth Bell (1988), Random House, New York, NY.

Coming Out to Parents by Mary V. Borhek (1983). Pilgrim Press, 132 West 31st St. New York, NY 10001.

Contrary to Love: Helping the Sexual Addict by Patrick Carnes (1989). CompCare Publishers, 2415 Annapolis Lane, Minneapolis, MN 55441, (800) 328-3330.

Out of the Shadows: The Sexual Addiction by Patrick Carnes (1983). CompCare Publishers, 2415 Annapolis Lane, Minneapolis, MN 55441, (800) 328-3330.

Top Secret—Sexual Assault Information for Teenagers Only by Jennifer Fay and Billie Jo Flerchinger (1985). Network Publications, P.O. Box 8506, Santa Cruz, CA 95061-8506, (408) 429-9822. Also available from King County Rape Relief, 305 S. 3rd, Renton, WA 98055, (206) 226-5062.

Shining Through: Pulling It Together After Sexual Abuse by Mindy B. Loiselle and Leslie Bailey Wright (1994). Safer Society Press, P.O. Box 340, Brandon, VT 05733-0340.

The Relapse Prevention Workbook for Youth in Treatment by Charlene Steen (1993). Safer Society Press, P.O. Box 340, Brandon, VT 05733-0340.

Who Am I & Why Am I in Treatment? A Guided Wookbook for Clients in Evaluation and Beginning Treatment by Robert Freeman-Longo and Laren Bays (1988). Safer Society Press, P.O. Box 340, Brandon, VT 05733-0340.

Why Did I Do It Again? Understanding My Cycle of Problem Behaviors by Laren Bays & Robert Freeman-Longo (1989). Safer Society Press, P.O. Box 340, Brandon, VT 05733-0340.

How Can I Stop? Breaking My Deviant Cycle by Laren Bays, Robert Freeman-Longo, & Diane Hildebran (1990). Safer Society Press, P.O. Box 340, Brandon, VT 05733-0340.

Empathy and Compassionate Action — Issues and Exercises: A Guided Workbook for Clients in Treatment by Robert E. Freeman-Longo, Laren Bays, & Euan Bear (1996). Safer Society Press, P.O. Box 340, Brandon, VT 05733-0340.

Men & Anger: Understanding and Managing Your Anger for a Much Better Life by Murray Cullen & Robert E. Freeman-Longo (1996). Safer Society Press, P.O. Box 340, Brandon, VT 05733-0340.

Boundaries: Where You End and I Begin by Ann Katharine (1991), Parkside Recovery Books, 205 West Touhy Avenue, Park Ridge, IL 60068, (800) 221-6364.

Secret Feelings and Thoughts: A Book About Male Victimization by Sexual Abuse by Rosemary Narimanian (1990). Philly Kids Play It Safe, 1650 Arch Street, 17th Floor, Suite 700, Philadelphia, PA 19103-1582, (215) 686-3966.

You Don't Have to Molest That Child by Timothy Smith (1987). National Committee for the Prevention of Child Abuse (NCPCA), Publishing Dept., 332 S. Michigan Ave., Suite 950, Chicago IL 60604-4357, (312) 663-3520.